SO-CDL-158

3 0050 01167 3463

DAN RATHER
And Other
Rough Drafts

BOOKS BY MARTHA ANNE TURNER

White Dawn Salutes Tomorrow
The City and Other Poems
Tools of the Earthmover
(Edited by Martha Anne Turner)
Sam Houston and His Twelve Women
The Life and Times of Jane Long
The Yellow Rose of Texas: The Story of a Song
William Barret Travis: His Sword and His Pen
Women of Texas
(In collaboration with others)
Texas Epic
The Yellow Rose of Texas: Her Saga and Her Song
Old Nacogdoches in the Jazz Age
Richard Bennett Hubbard: An American Life
Clara Driscoll: An American Tradition
The World of Colonel John W. Thomason USMC
Dan Rather and Other Rough Drafts

DAN RATHER
And Other
Rough Drafts

Martha Anne Turner

E. H. Antone ★ Monte Barrett ★ Mody Boatright
Jewel Gibson ★ J. Evetts Haley ★ Carl Hertzog
Charles Lee Hill ★ C. L. Sonnichsen
Walter Prescott Webb ★ Patsy Woodall

EAKIN PRESS
Austin, Texas

Library of Congress Cataloging-in-Publication Data

Turner, Martha Anne.
    Dan Rather and other rough drafts.

    Bibliography: p.
    Includes index.
    1. Texas — Biography. I. Title. II. Title: Dan Rather and other rough drafts.
CT262.T87   1987   920'.0764   87-1618
ISBN 0-89015-501-1

To the memory of Louise Gilchrist
This volume is dedicated

Contents

Foreword

Author Martha Anne Turner not only observed and admired the people who influenced her life in some manner; she cemented their contributions by converting her appreciation into the written word.

Whether her relationship with the person was peripheral or lifelong, she brings each into closer focus so that we feel as if we, too, have spent some time with each dynamic personality.

The contributions of each are diverse. But be they folklorist, historian, news correspondent, bookmaker, author, musician, or indefatigable citizen, their influence on Texas, the Southwest — even the world, in some cases — illustrates a unity in devotion to a profession and in service to humanity.

The writing of this collection of essays spanned several years. Some of the essays were previously printed in other publications, some were presented as speeches by the author, others were written expressly for this book. Several of the subjects have died since the time the author etched segments of their lives into these pages.

The author herself did not outlive the publication of this book. Perhaps then, while applauding the characters that we meet in these "rough drafts," we should add Martha Anne Turner to this select crowd of those who merit recognition.

MELISSA LOCKE ROBERTS
Editor

Preface

In a certain sense this book is an inventory. In another, it is an expression of appreciation. The persons portrayed here, some no longer living, have related to my professional career, some more closely and more significantly than others. Highly productive people, they have made this confused nuclear world habitable.

Dan Rather I knew as a student on the campus of Sam Houston State University. The university takes no credit for the success of the CBS anchorman. But we are happy that Dan came our way. Indeed he could very well have been a product of Yale or Harvard, but you don't hitchhike that far away from Houston with empty pockets. Dan represents Texas well. Moreover, unlike some people today who make it to the top, he remembers the friends who smiled and waved to him along the way.

Jewel Gibson, one of two women I include in this book, is in a class to herself. I knew Jewel (whose name is eminently appropriate) both as a student and fellow faculty member of the English Department at Sam Houston. She returned to the campus to complete her academic work after her first taste of literary success. Few people have influenced me in the same way as Jewel. She has been an inspiration to me for something like four decades.

It is not an exaggeration to say that Patsy Woodall — the other woman gracing my book — is one of the most fascinating persons I've ever known. She's been everywhere, done everything, and rubbed shoulders with many of the great of our time. Now in her nineties, she demonstrates a zest for living that is no less than phenomenal. Knowing her has enriched and broadened my philosophy.

To say that only two of these people were my teachers — Walter Prescott Webb and Mody Boatright — would not be entirely accurate. I did enroll in courses on the graduate level taught by Webb and Boatright. But all of these friends helped to shape what I am.

ix

Even Dan Rather taught me to place a higher premium on the dignity of labor and honest effort.

Webb and Boatright were associated with my alma mater, The University of Texas at Austin. Webb was one of the finest minds I ever came in contact with, even though he was not, when I knew him, a dynamic professor. On the other hand, Boatright, whom I knew as instructor and employer (he awarded me graduate fellowships as I earned my master of arts degree), was not only impeccable around the seminar table, he was a person of rare warmth and charisma. I first became acquainted with Dr. Boatright when he served as my supervisory professor for the creative project *The City and Other Poems,* which I was permitted to submit in lieu of the traditional thesis for my degree.

While I met the late Monte Barrett and J. Evetts Haley at a writers conference, I came to know each better through his works, especially the latter, whose Southwestern classics I incorporated into the format of a course I taught at Sam Houston called Literature of the Southwest. Haley and I also shared The University of Texas as student and teacher.

Three others who contributed to my writing career were Carl Hertzog, E. H. Antone, and C. L. Sonnichsen — a powerful creative triad formerly attached to the University of Texas at El Paso. Hertzog and Antone published my first book on the Yellow Rose of Texas, and Sonnichsen wrote an introduction to my latest treatment of the subject, *The Yellow Rose of Texas: Her Saga and Her Song.*

Charles Lee Hill is another friend I knew at Sam Houston State. Hill became a legend in the music world before he was forty. Today his compositions "Space City, USA" and "At the Gremlin Ball" are better known in Europe than in America.

I read the Rather sketch in an abridged form at a professional meeting sponsored by Texas A&M University in the spring of 1983. The article "Joshua Beene and Jewel Gibson" appeared in the *Journal of the American Studies Association of Texas* for 1979. The Boatright profile was read in an abbreviated version at the annual convention of the American Studies Association of Texas at Port Arthur in November 1983 and was published in the ASAT *Journal* for 1984. The Haley portrait was published in the Fall 1984 issue of *The Texas Review.* These articles are reprinted here by permission.

I make grateful acknowledgment to my friends for their patience in answering my queries and for sharing with me essential material.

I am also indebted to the library staff of Sam Houston State University, particularly Charles L. Dwyer, for research assistance. My thanks go also to my secretary, Jeanette Koger; my photographer, Westen McCoy; and my publisher, Ed Eakin of Eakin Press, Austin.

MARTHA ANNE TURNER
1985

The Real Dan Rather: Television's Eight-Million-Dollar Man

In 1949, when Dan Rather hitchhiked to the campus of Sam Houston State Teachers College from Houston, he was a hungry, street-smart city kid with stardust in his eyes. Today the tough, hard-hitting image the anchorman of "CBS Evening News" projects is a professional stance of control and assurance he acquired from thirty years of hard work.

And if Rather's climb to the top was not meteoric, neither was it pedestrian. After graduating from Sam Houston in 1953, he gained rugged experience as a United States Marine for a brief space, then joined radio station KTRH, an affiliate of the *Houston Chronicle*.[1] He switched to television five years later, and in 1961 became anchorman for KHOU, Houston affiliate of CBS.[2] His photographing of Hurricane Carla in September 1961 thrust him into the national news forefront.[3] In 1962 he accepted the post as chief of the CBS news bureau in Dallas and won additional distinction in his coverage of the assassination of President John F. Kennedy in 1963.[4]

He was named the White House correspondent for CBS in 1964 and was transferred to the network's London bureau the following year.[5] Returning to Washington in 1966, he remained at the

1

national capital through 1974. Following Watergate, Rather was assigned to "CBS Reports," the network's documentary series.[6]

It was on March 19, 1974, that an incident in Houston focused the national spotlight on Rather. President Nixon and his entourage were in the process of taking their defense of Nixon's involvement in Watergate to the people. Houston, Rather's former hometown, was on their itinerary.[7]

At a press conference, Nixon responded to a Watergate question by stating that he had fully complied with the demands of the grand jury and the special prosecutor's office. Rather challenged the president's statement with a two-part question. In the controversial exchange, Nixon, either to confuse or squelch the CBS correspondent, countered with "Are you running for something?"

Rather's answer, "No, sir, Mr. President, are you?" has become a journalism classic.[8]

In 1975, when "60 Minutes" moved into prime time, Rather became one of the three permanent correspondents for the news series.[9] Then, in 1981, Dan Rather stepped up to the most prestigious position in television news to succeed CBS anchorman Walter Cronkite, an acknowledged legend and an almost impossible act to follow.[10]

When Rather took a degree in journalism in 1953 from Sam Houston State Teachers College (now Sam Houston State University), the standard answer to the question "Who are the two biggest men on campus?" was "President Harmon Lowman and Dan Rather." [11]

But Dan Rather did not become a BMOC overnight. He served a lean apprenticeship during his freshman year. When the naive eighteen-year-old, fresh out of Houston's Reagan High School, matriculated at Sam Houston in the fall of 1949, his mother cashed in two twenty-five-dollar government bonds (each worth only $18.75) to pay his fees.[12] After registration, he probably had less than ten dollars with which to face the future.

At least Dan could depend temporarily on Bearkat Den, the football squad dormitory, for a roof over his head. Moreover, he could feed from the same free trough as the other aspirants to gridiron fame. When Rather hitchhiked to the campus earlier to apply for an athletic scholarship from the legendary coach, the all-time

Texas A&M great Puny Wilson,[13] the latter, noncommittal and flinty, did not flatly reject him. Neither did he encourage him. Still Dan, who had had a taste of high school football, was hopeful of making the team. Wilson permitted the candidate from Houston to suit up three times. After observing him at the last workout, Wilson delivered his ultimatum.

"Son, I watched ya out thar the whole time t'day," Wilson informed Dan, his fish eyes squinting to mere slits. "And I wanna tellya sump'in . . . You're little [Rather weighed 150] and you're *yellow!* [14]

That summer Rather got a job with a pipeline crew, digging ditches, as his father, a construction worker, had done before him.[15] Reinforced with what to him was the astronomical sum of $200 he had managed to squirrel away, he returned to the campus for the fall semester of 1950, prepared to conquer the world. Thus planted and watered, he began to bloom. Dan Rather bloomed like nothing else the school named for the hero of San Jacinto had witnessed since its founding in 1879.

The oldest of three children, Rather had grown up with an ingrained respect for work. No task was too menial for him. He would tackle anything, short of committing a felony, to earn a buck. He waited tables, pumped gas, washed cars, slung hash. He worked before breakfast. He worked in the afternoons, worked between classes, and frequently all night long on weekends.

He edited the biweekly campus paper, *The Houstonian,* corresponded for the town weekly, *The Huntsville Item,* handled college publicity for the state press, and became a stringer for the wire services.

But the job that converted Dan Rather's name into a household word on the local horizon was his employment with Huntsville's radio station KSAM.[16] Pronounced *Kay Sam* and categorized as a teakettle, the station consisted of a three-room shack, with a tower in the back, and an outhouse with an antenna on top. The station's operating power was 250 watts.

The way Dan obtained the job was unusual. With preliminary questions and answers out of the way, the owner of the station, a Baptist preacher and frustrated journalist, asked Dan if he had ever covered any football games play-by-play.

Dan had not but felt that he could. "Go ahead and give me a sample," the preacher urged.

Using the Sam Houston Bearkats and a fictitious opposing team, Dan did six minutes. It helped that he had fantasized a broadcast of a roller derby en route to the campus one day and on another had imagined the blow-by-blow details of an apocryphal football game in which he had made a spectacular end run to score the winning touchdown with only two seconds left to play.

The KSAM job was a one-man operation. Rather did the newscasts, the commercials, and broadcast all the athletic contests — the junior high, senior high, and black high school (no integration then) football and basketball games — in addition to college sports, all reported play-by-play. The fact was he became so proficient that ticket sales fell off.

Nor did his duties end there. He fought a losing battle with the telephone (business calls, smart alecs challenging his facts, others correcting his grammar and pronunciation, housewives seeking information). He kept the outmoded equipment in repair, cut the grass, painted the tower, and did anything else that his employer, who prided himself on being a man of the cloth, could think of — all for the pittance of forty cents an hour.

On weekends Rather reported to the radio station by 6:00 in the morning and worked without a break until midnight. Except for the convenience long-playing records provided, he sometimes went for hours without eating. At least once during the Gospel Hour, which allowed sixty minutes of free time from 8:00 to 9:00 at night, his trip to town for a hamburger proved to be unfortunate. Usually, he drove the two miles to town in the Mobile News Unit, a 1937 Plymouth pickup truck, ordered his food to go, and ate it at the station. This time, however, there was a new waitress whose proportions impressed Dan, and he decided to eat at the hamburger stand and flirt with her. She, like himself, was a student working her way through Sam Houston . . .

The man of the cloth reached his employee by telephone after several attempts to locate him.

"Have you heard my radio station in the last twenty minutes?" the incensed minister demanded.

"Well, er, no, sir. You see, I ran out for a quick sandwich and, er, got detained."

"Then get your butt where you can hear it," the man of the cloth ordered. "Get back to the station . . . fix it . . . and you're fired."

Dan rushed out to the truck and turned on the radio. The long-playing record was stuck. For thirty minutes Bible Belt Huntsville had been hearing what sounded out of context like "GO TO HELL . . . GO TO HELL . . . GO TO HELL." [17]

But as time-consuming as the job was, it had its lateral compensations. For instance, a romantic college girl would occasionally join Rather during the Gospel Hour and the couple would desert hymns and homily for a private romp in the back room.

When did this young human dynamo have time to study? Undoubtedly, he snatched odd moments during and between recordings, between newscasts and commercials, most of which he wrote, and after midnight.

While Rather thrived on activity, none of it interfered with his academic standing. He made the dean's list for three successive years and graduated in the top quarter of a class of 336. His rating in the Journalism Department was tops. He was named to Alpha Chi, honorary scholarship fraternity, in 1951–52, and was awarded a grant for outstanding literary achievement in 1952–53. In his senior year, he was listed in *Who's Who in American Colleges and Universities*.[18]

What was Rather really like as a student? In the classroom, he was the essence of courtesy. But he had a curious mind that prompted him to ask more questions than the average student. Skeptical of an instructor's line of thought, he did not hesitate to question him. On the other hand, if he were called upon and unprepared, he simply stated that he did not know the answer. Some of Dan's buddies claimed that, after a night of work, when he had not had the opportunity to study, he would slip into his seat as unobtrusively as possible and keep his head down in order to appear inconspicuous.

Underneath his collegiate trappings and that incredible energy that drove him so furiously in pursuit of a goal, there was another face of Dan Rather. This Dan Rather excelled as a human being. This was the boy who cried when Coach Wilson rejected him for the football team. This was the student who rescued an inebriated classmate from the top of Huntsville's high water tower.[19] This was the Dan Rather who influenced more than one classmate to stay in school and lent him money.

In 1950, when Rather, scarcely nineteen, was a sophomore, he left a permanent record of this aspect of his personality. It was in the nature of a short story — Rather's first serious attempt at creativity — published in the campus literary magazine which I sponsored.[20] I recognized at the time that the young writer was extraordinarily gifted. The clean, clipped, staccato style for which he is noted today is evident in that initial specimen of his writing.[21] But what impressed me more than the story's literary merit was the portrait that it revealed of Dan Rather.

Entitled "The Sale," the story is a Christmas piece in which a young clerk has an experience that teaches him the true meaning of the anniversary of the Savior's birth. As Christmas Eve, the final day of his employment, nears an end, the clerk realizes that his sales are slightly less than the amount necessary to win a hundred-dollar bonus.

Shortly before the closing bell rings, a customer approaches. The customer is a seedy-looking man who desires to purchase a stove. The stove has been ordered by his sick child's doctor, and the only requirement is that it must have the capacity to heat the fifteen-by-forty-foot room inhabited by the family in the city slums. The indigent customer does not have enough money to pay for a stove large enough to produce the necessary heat.

Consequently, the salesman, in order to qualify for the bonus, misrepresents the capability of a cheaper model.

Later, the salesman, in his exuberance at qualifying for the bonus, knocks over and breaks the figurines of the Nativity scene displayed close by. In the midst of the broken pieces on the floor is the pink sales slip. Not until he has rushed out into the street filled now with the melodic sounds of Christmas and hurrying last-minute shoppers does the salesman, still clutching the telltale slip, realize the enormity of his selfishness. He returns to the store, has the bookkeeper, busy over his ledgers, charge him with the more expensive heater, and rushes out to make the delivery himself.

When forty-seven-year-old Dan Rather, Emmy Award-winning CBS correspondent and author of two bestsellers — *The Palace Guard* and *The Camera Never Blinks* — returned to the Sam Houston

State University campus on October 21, 1977, as one of four distinguished alumni to be honored at the annual homecoming,[22] he requested that I send him a copy of the story. He said that it meant a great deal to him.

Rather maintains close contact with his alma mater and his friends in Texas. Supportive of Sam Houston State University's Alumni Association, he has paid annual VIP membership dues of $500 for several years, and he recently donated $15,000 to the organization's scholarship fund.[23]

The CBS anchorman is easily accessible by telephone unless he is absent from his New York base on assignment.[24] When he is absent, his pleasant assistant, Susan Schackman, acts as his surrogate, handling mail and personal calls.

An innately modest person, Rather insists that he is still a reporter and does not expect to be detached from the field in the role of anchorman. As he puts it, "Being laid back is not my style. I don't think that's Dan Rather, and I hope it never is." [25]

Asked why the CBS television network chose him for the post, Rather said he honestly didn't know. He hastened to explain, however:

> The people that made the decision said that the biggest factor was experience. They were looking for the person with the widest variety of experience under the toughest circumstances and who had demonstrated he could handle a lot of different kinds of assignments under pressure. . . . We've got a number of people that fit that category. I'm not under any illusions. I know that I'm not the only person that can do the job.

Rather recalls his Watergate confrontation with Richard Nixon without rancor. In fact, he insists that he was only doing his job.

"I think the record is very clear," he said. "I never baited Richard Nixon. Yes, I have thought about it and no, I don't know how else it could have been done." [26] Many people accept Rather's explanation of this today — the same people who would have branded it as brash fabrication a few years ago.

The CBS newscaster has his own ground rules for the assessment of news anchors. They are precisely what you would expect. "On big breaking stories does he or she do it well? Does he or she have command and authority over the daily news? And, when you see the evening news, is it the best?" [27]

Since Hurricane Carla, Rather has proved his expertise on covering on-the-spot news. As a reporter for KHOU-TV, he not only tracked the progress of the three-day storm from his base in Galveston (on a mobile truck where his equipment was set up), but also photographed Carla and televised it superimposed on a map of the Texas coast and Gulf of Mexico.

I can see him now. As Dan talked, he tapped the screen with a pointer, his youthful voice unwavering and proud:

"There it is folks," he said. "Never before seen on television live, an actual hurricane — Carla, the biggest of this century." And indeed there it was, all 400 lethal miles of it — a crescent-shaped cyclone, coming straight at us from the tube, with a fifty-mile-wide eye resembling a gargantuan doughnut.[28]

The feat of photographing Carla live moved Rather into a TV correspondent's slot in New York, and the TV journalist will tell you today that, with the exception of his wife Jean, the lady that had the most influence on his career was named Carla.

Rather collected additional laurels for his skill in handling a breaking story when he anchored CBS's coverage of the royal wedding of Prince Charles and Lady Diana Spencer in London.

One television editor made this report:

> CBS has run its string as the No. 1 network in prime time to 11 weeks . . . according to figures from the A. C. Nielsen Co.
>
> The wedding in London of Prince Charles and Lady Diana Spencer dominated the original programming offered by the networks in the week ending August 2, but only one of five pre- and post-wedding specials was on CBS.
>
> CBS listed four of the week's 10 highest rated shows . . . and compiled an average rating for the period of 14.5, to 13.6 for ABC and 12.2 for NBC.[29]

Is Rather in command? That question has already been answered, but additional detail is warranted here. Naturally, Rather was glad when he no longer was labeled Cronkite's successor. According to a *TV Guide* article by Sally Bedell, Dan Rather has more than made it on his own.

"Rather has clearly taken command of the program, and already he has proved to be different from Cronkite, who remained aloof and intimidating. Rather deals directly with the troops, often screening tapes and offering helpful suggestions." [30]

For that matter, he considers his job as managing editor more important than being anchor of the "Evening News." Sometimes he devotes twelve hours a day to it and frequently omits lunch when he's engrossed in his work. Following each broadcast, he meets with his top producers to talk over the next day's assignments. He also likes to discuss details and invites suggestions for the improvement of coverage.

As for the "Evening News with Dan Rather" being the best, the anchorman is dedicated to it. Rather himself believed that it would take a year, or perhaps a year and a half, for the program to stabilize. His phenomenal progress indicates that he was wrong. It is common knowledge that the program stabilized in less than a year.

But some of Rather's detractors are still at work. They charge him with being too contrived, too rehearsed. Rather attributes this to the fact that he believes in preparation. He does his homework.

Before anchoring CBS's coverage of the space shuttle, he devoted six hours a night for two weeks to reading briefing books and additional informative material. For comparative purposes, he has also studied tapes of his predecessors' broadcasts and films of them at work.

Critics fault Dan for not having written his two books without assistance. They never stop to think of the long hours he expends on the job per se. On "60 Minutes" alone, Rather frequently worked on five stories at a time and logged 100 hours per week on the job. The travel his assignments necessitated was in itself time-consuming. Dan became a cosmopolite in pursuit of stories. He hardly had time to recover from one siege of jet lag before beginning another flight. At least once, Rather did an interview on an airport runway in sixteen minutes before the pilot took off.

Rather admits that his first year was tough. Now that the pressure has eased up somewhat, he looks back on it as "the silly season" when the critics reviewed everything: his hair, his sweater, his manner. But at the end of his second year, he takes it all philosophically in stride.

"Don't be crushed if you fail. If you allow yourself to be crushed . . . then you'll never put yourself in a pressure situation again, and you'll never grow." [31]

He even goes so far as to make a list of positive things to do to combat pressure — a list too long to include here but which tells us that Dan Rather still has the answers.

Rather tends to shield his private life from the limelight. Not often do you see the names of the Rather children in the press: the daughter Robin and the son Daniel, both in their twenties. His svelte and attractive wife, the former Jean Goebel, a native Texan like himself, shares his interests: reading, the theater, travel, fishing. She is also intensely interested in his career. "More than anyone else," Rather says, "she understands my hopes and my dreams." [32]

Perhaps the finest demonstration of Jean's understanding of Dan's hopes and dreams came during those days when he was sweating out the decision as to which anchor job to take.

Certainly, it was not an easy choice to make. "I find myself in a long final glide path," *Time* quoted Rather as saying. "Three runways are stretched out before me. All three beautiful. I could land on any one and be extremely happy." [33]

But Jean was patient as she empathized with her husband in his struggle. Finally, after two weeks of agonizing, there came that last day when Dan told her he would decide. Faithful Jean reminded him of his promise and also, if he intended keeping it, that he had "only 17 minutes left." [34]

"I am going with my gut," Dan told her. "I'm going with CBS." [35]

So Dan Rather went with his gut, *Time* magazine carried the cover story, and CBS, after two years, knows what a bargain their eight-million-dollar man is.

Joshua Beene and Jewel Gibson

Sixty-one years after Mark Twain's *Adventures of Huckleberry Finn* was banned in Boston in 1885, Jewel Gibson's *Joshua Beene And God* was condemned in more than one Texas town. One Baptist minister denounced the novel from his pulpit and proposed burning it. Circumspect Boston thought the unwashed and unschooled picaro Huck Finn — son of the town drunk — would corrupt the morals of the city's youth. In the protesting Texas hamlets, any book that pointed an accusing finger was offensive. Moreover, it was the hide-bound shepherd's duty to warn his unsuspecting flock against what to him was insidious blasphemy: a book focusing on an aging patriarch — a self-appointed, egocentric messiah and collaborator of the Almighty intent upon expelling sin from Spring Creek.

The rejections, despite the separation of years, demonstrate the existence of that very bigotry and insularity which both books hold up to ridicule as they confirm that prejudice is no respecter of either time or people.

What is more, in 1946 — the year of the release of *Joshua Beene And God* — the world had not recovered from the shock of the anthropomorphic god Adolph Hitler played in exterminating in Ger-

11

man-occupied Europe six million Jews. Despite the defeat of the
man who played God in 1945, Hitler inaugurated a new era in
which power and violence became commonplace and people began
to lament the death of a triune deity. (The recent Jonestown,
Guiana, tragedy was a manifestation of this confused culture.)

Meanwhile, as the myopic continued to protest Mrs. Gibson's
satire of the impact of antropomorphism on Christianity, discern-
ing readers and critics alike hailed her first novel, published in
America by Bennett Cerf of Random House in 1946 and abroad by
Eyre & Spottiswoode of London in 1948, as a literary feast. Applause from the homefront was particularly satisfying.

Paul Crume of the *Dallas Morning News* compared the novel
with the work of George Sessions Perry. "*Joshua Beene And God* is a
novel of Texas that has more fidelity than any other novel dealing
with Texas material since George Sessions Perry published *Hold
Autumn in Your Hand*." [1] This was high praise as Perry's novel of the
East Texas tenant farmer won the Texas Institute of Letters award
for 1941, along with unanimous national acclaim. Even more significant, Crume credited Mrs. Gibson with more authenticity in
her treatment of Texas materials than Perry. He also felt that the
author's humor of social criticism compared with the best of Er-
skine Caldwell. He pointed out that Mrs. Gibson's employment of
a technique of "maneuvering moral platitudes into humor" was
reminiscent of Caldwell. Furthermore, Crume was convinced that
in *Joshua Beene And God* the author had achieved "something good
and something honest, and a good many people who have been
writing and trying for years have not been able to do as much." [2]

Sigman Byrd, contemporary author and *Houston Post* book editor, who called the novel "mercilessly profound," also compared it
with the writings of Perry and Roark Bradford, creator of John
Henry. He believed Mrs. Gibson's work to be "infinitely more
caustic and penetrating" than that of either. Equally important,
Byrd predicted that for every sanctimonious friend Jewel Gibson
lost over the publication, she would acquire a hundred honest ad-
mirers.

The commissioning of the late J. Frank Dobie, native Texan
and author of national magnitude, to review the novel for the *Chicago Daily Sun* was in itself a good omen. Dobie declared that it was
"the pulsation of the juices of life" that give *Joshua Beene And God* vi-

tality. He likened Josh, in his ability "to call down a death on a man" and raise the dead, to the Mexican hero in Frank Goodwyn's *The Magic of Limping John*. Like the Goodwyn novel, Mrs. Gibson's was, he said, a burlesque not only on the narrow littleness of Spring Creek yokels — "as H. L. Mencken used to call this class of people — and Jewel Gibson views them considerably in the Mencken manner" [3] — but also of the idea of their credulity in the prophet himself.

But the dean of Southwestern folklore found no burlesque in the earthy idiom of the characters. Rather, he commended the author for her skill in the art of writing.

Although Anne Calhoun of the *Dallas Times-Herald* predicted that Mrs. Gibson's novel would shock some people, she stated that those people who base religious tolerance and development more on intellect than raw emotion would accept the work as "a clearly focused photograph of religious fanaticism." [4] Mrs. Calhoun asserted further: "This is a book for anyone who is not ashamed to be reminded that facts are facts, right or wrong. This was Texas — it still may be Texas in isolated spots." [5]

The *Houston Chronicle* appraised *Joshua Beene And God* "as a book of originality and authentic merit." [6] Further, it admitted that "in *Joshua Beene And God* Mrs. Gibson has created a classically sincere religious fanatic, an unconscionable bigot whose outrageous pontificating and preposterous conceit is satirically the most powerful inveighment against intolerance, narrow-mindedness, and hypocrisy printed . . . in a long, long time." [7]

Perhaps it was to be expected that the author's contemporaries in Texas might incline to higher assessment of her first effort than critics of national reputation. Nevertheless, almost without exception, veteran critics and bookmen of the nation's outstanding periodicals were equally voluble in their acceptance. Uniformly, they extolled the author's initial offering for its originality, excellent characterization, and superb satire, along with other noteworthy disciplines.

None was more articulate than Thomas Sugrue of the *New York Herald Tribune*, to whom the novel was "good hard cider . . . hard to beat." [8] He pronounced it excellent as a first novel, recognized it as "a first class piece of Americana, a superb satire on the ultimate degeneration of anthropomorphism." Furthermore,

Joshua Beene is no wild freak; he has lived all over the United States and is by no means dead and gone. But, beyond this, Joshua's story is delightful entertainment; the other characters are as real as he, though not as rascally . . . The Texas setting is evoked with sure tender strokes; the woodland scenes are as lovely as Joshua's beard . . . a great man, Joshua, and unto him Mrs. Gibson has rendered what is due.[9]

In the conservative *Saturday Review* Phil Stong assessed the novel as a "really masterly job of transplanting the damnations of the prophets of older Palestine to present Texas." Furthermore, Stong saw the protagonist as "a blackmailing prophet . . . a kind of Old Man of the Tribe." [10]

The *New York Times* observed that "The background of American revivalism has always produced rich characters" and cited Joshua Beene as no exception. The *Times* praised the author for "an excellently rounded characterization." [11]

While Jesse E. Cross in the *Library Journal* found the novel to be "humorous — but surprisingly reverent," Pamela Hansford Johnson of London, who reviewed the English edition in *John O'London's Weekly,* saluted its "gigantic structure" and proclaimed it to be "something unique in American fiction . . . by a writer with a distinctive and authoritative voice." [12]

Any controversial publication inspires legend. *Joshua Beene And God* is no exception. One with some basis in fact concerns an old fifty-cent piece dated 1876 which the author found when she was a child. She preserved the coin as a talisman without attaching importance to it. Later, when she was called to New York for a conference with her publishers, she ran across the coin and observed that Miss Liberty was sitting down.

She showed it to her husband, who had it mounted as a pin and suggested that she wear it to New York — home of the standing Miss Liberty — for luck.

Publicity stimulated a few stories. When the attractive, grayhaired, vivacious author — mother of two grown sons and a grandmother at forty — saw her photograph in the *Dallas Times-Herald,* she commented, "The Dallas people have been wonderful to me, but the newspaper photographer there struck me below the third chin!"

Other legends circulated after the book's release. Upon seeing a copy for the first time, a close friend, who recognized herself in one of the characters, vowed to the author, "I'll never speak to you again!" It was rumored that Mrs. Gibson's mother scolded her for not being a good Baptist and for favoring the Campbellites in *Joshua Beene And God*. Asked if he had the novel in stock, the proprietor of a religious bookstore answered succinctly that the store did not and — what was more — never would have.

But the legend that swept the country from coast to coast was this one. A book jobber, astonished that the publishers could scarcely satisfy the demand for the book — a success that he had not foreseen — said: "I can sell a funny book, and I can sell a religious book. But I'll be damned if I can sell a funny, religious book!" [13]

Two theatrical productions of the novel increased its audience in the fifties and sixties. In the first, Houston's Alley Theater opened its 1950–51 season with a fifteen-performance run. The novel, a natural for conversion into folk drama because of its authentic folk material and episodic style, was adapted to the stage by Clifford Sage and Hal Lewis, two Dallas newspapermen. Alley Theater director Nina Vance produced the play. Jerome Jordan, veteran actor and producer from Dallas and former associate of David Belasco of Broadway, portrayed the role of Josh with professional polish and excellent timing. The novelist herself was persuaded by Miss Vance to play the part of Phoebe Goolsby. Director-producer Vance tailored the scenes effectively for exhibition in the Alley's theater in the round, and the comedy-drama had an enormously successful run.

Twelve years later, the Repertory Company of Dallas launched its 1961–62 season with a revival of the play in which the international show business figure and folksinger Burl Ives starred. Staged in the Dallas Theater Center, the play represented one of the major productions of the noted director Paul Baker. Later, Baker staged premieres of Mrs. Gibson's two early dramatic successes — *Miss Ney* and *Brann: The Iconoclast*.

Joshua Beene And God has been categorized as a regional novel. However, several factors argue with the classification. Foremost among these is the novel's international acceptance as an American classic and its wide appeal in the nation itself. Another is that the novel not only has catholicity — like all good writing, irrespective of labels — but is an exception to the regional culture area concept — a basically ecological construct. As one writer illustrates the point: "A beef stew by a cook in San Antonio, Texas, may have a different flavor from that of a beef stew cooked in Pittsburgh, Pennsylvania, but the essential substances of potatoes and onions, with some suggestion of beef, are about the same, and geography has no effect on their digestibility." [14]

These essential ingredients prevent the novel from being regional. Inasmuch as the novel transcends the geographical limitations and sociocultural areas of regionalism, a more accurate classification is that of folk literature. While *Joshua Beene And God* is at once a powerful satire that castigates religious astigmatism rooted in a locale tainted with race prejudice and ignorance, the novel fulfills admirably the requisites of the folktale.

Although the term "folktale" originally applied to the complex so-called "fairy tale" peculiar to children's literature, there is no reason to ignore recent folktales that have more believable plots and true-to-life characters. Not only have these recent types of folktales replaced the fairy tales in most American and in many foreign oral traditions, but they have also inspired the writing of folk drama and fiction incorporating fundamental elements of the genre, such as customs, idiom, attitudes, and environmental difficulties of the folk, who tend to be credible and live close to the soil and to nature.[15] *Joshua Beene And God* is such a novel.

Although the locale of Spring Creek was said to represent a composite Texas town and bears the stamp of a number of places involving Mrs. Gibson's teaching career, the fact remains that it evolved almost literally from a hamlet in Robertson County, where the author was born and grew up. Tucked away in the northeastern corner of the county on a bare site between Duck and Steele creeks, Bald Prairie, twelve miles east of Bremond, was established in 1865, according to *The Handbook of Texas*, and was named for its stark location.[16]

However, typescripts by Alta Rae Reagan, a local historian and descendant of one of the founders, asserts that the community had an earlier origin and was named for Henry Bald.[17] Born in 1904, the novelist found no difficulty in reverting to the last decade before the turn of the century — scarcely fourteen years — for an arbitrary time pattern since the very location of the rural village gave it distinction and removed it from the erosion of so-called civilized centers.

Robertson County, christened for the colonizer Sterling C. Robertson, was organized as early as 1838. But Southern planters — migrating essentially from western Tennessee, Mississippi, Alabama, and Georgia — were attracted before that time by the fertile riverbottom lands conducive to the production of cotton. These pioneers put down deep roots.[18] Indeed, some of them crossed the Mississippi to settle in Texas while it was still under Spanish rule and remained to take part in the Texas Revolution that ended Mexican sovereignty in 1836. Others fought for the Confederacy in the Civil War.

No doubt the choice of Spring Creek as the setting was prompted by Spring, a diminutive town near Houston, where Mrs. Gibson was employed at the time of the novel's release. But unmistakable are the intimate scenes in *Joshua Beene And God* reflective of the author's childhood — those along Duck Creek, on whose banks Jehovah's Oak is located, the old Church of Christ, and the cemetery surrounding it. The Church of Christ building that figures prominently in the story is still intact and displays a historical medallion for being the oldest of the denomination in the state. The little cemetery, reminiscent of Stoke Poges in Grey's "Elegy Written in a Country Churchyard" and the burial place of many of the community's old settlers and heroes from three wars, has met the encroachments of time with singular resistance. The native flora and fauna that had largely escaped the lethal pruning hook and sportsman's gun and that serve as the recurring leitmotiv of the novel, on the other hand, have succumbed to the incursions of both time and progress.

The protagonist Joshua Beene himself is a character to adorn a tall tale, a folk hero that could have been scissored from the whole cloth of seventeenth-century religious folklore. His faith in his own supernatural faculties emanating directly from God — the talent to bring down a curse on his enemies and the power to resurrect the dead — find basis in the doctrines and practices of the Massachusetts Bay Colony. Colonial theocrats used their claims for such powers as protective devices against heretics in their midst and outside influences threatening the Puritan state.[19]

Joshua Beene employs his claims, at the outset of the novel, as vehicles to oppose the Baptists — his and God's arch antagonists — who are a menace to his supremacy as messiah and political boss of Spring Creek. Moreover, since he feels co-equal with God, Uncle Josh ascribes to himself, like the seventeenth-century theocrats, the same phenomenal powers. Thus, again in the manner of the colonial divines, the prophet demands that he and his collaborator combine their efforts to destroy their enemies.

Another strong link with religious folklore of the American Colonial period, and inextricably related to the former aspect, is Joshua's belief in the revelation of God's will through natural or secondary causes. The seventeenth-century zealot was convinced that God provided clues to His will, that is, His revelation of holy wrath or divine favor, through transpirings, or providences, in nature.[20] Thus thunderstorms, floods, and unusual accidents and other disasters were providences of damnation reflecting disfavor, whereas all wonderful deliverances of the afflicted or distressed and mercies extended to the godly were expressions of divine approval. The judgment of a curse typified a providence of damnation; the act of raising the dead signified one of divine favor.

Though Uncle Josh maintains direct and audible communication with God, the Almighty exhorts him to seek further instruction from manifestations and symbolic meanings in nature. For instance, at the beginning of the novel God exhorts:

> I trust you, Joshua. Now, you just open your eyes and look around you. Not only have I given you plenty of Scriptures to read, but I've given you the ant to watch and the honeybee . . .[21]

Then, as Uncle Josh surveys the landscape, the familiar surroundings assume new significance:

> The very oak, under which he had many times talked to the Lord, became a sort of symbol. There on the banks of the creek, its giant roots in the water, it stood in spite of the grapevine that clung to it for support and the moss that dangled from its branches. To Uncle Josh the stream symbolized the River of Life; the oak, the Church of Christ; the moss, the sins that soiled its members.[22]

But *Joshua Beene And God* has much more to say about the earthy folk of the rural Texas village of the horse-and-buggy era than its religious overtones imply. Uncorrupted by twentieth-century speed and space-age machines, citizens of Spring Creek developed a manual resourcefulness alien to today's computerized and push-button society. Keepers of the barnyard and the pasture, tillers of the soil, the citizens produced their own food and harvested their crops with hands made callous and with backs bowed from long hours of labor. The author recalls having picked cotton at the age of five and chopped cotton with a blue-handled hoe — an award from her proud father — by her tenth birthday. Spring Creek citizens cooked their meals on wood-burning stoves, drew water from wells equipped with bucket and pulley, burned oil lamps, and managed to exist without the luxury of modern plumbing.

Yet in their very ruggedness and primitive lifestyle they are beautiful — and immoral. The inhabitants of Spring Creek are beautiful and sinful as they go about their daily communication with one another. They destroy character; they cheat in business deals; they commit adultery. The prophet himself is not above lusting after the body of Phoebe while she is still the wife of Elmer Goolsby, whose death he anticipates with pleasure. The greedy Elmer, who is slow to pay his debts, charges small boys a nickel each — their Sunday school offering — to ride to church in his flashy new wagon.

Furthermore, as provincial as much of the material of the novel seems, the author's sophisticated treatment makes adroit use of folk customs characteristic of the era. Examples are the expulsion of church members for an infraction of the religious code or a violation of a civil offense unacceptable to the community, the pitching of a hymn at the graveside funeral service, the neighborly practice of constructing a pine box in which to bury the dead, and the distinctive Spring Creek dialect.

No amount of nineteenth-century education could corrupt the dialect's purity. New linguistic habits, like "them rediculous-lookin' bathin' togs," are for the young, and Joshua Beene is a past master of the dialectic rhythms, particularly in his conferences with God:

> They're a-plum spoilin' the looks of Spring Creek — a-picnickin' and a-pickin' the flowers, A-comin' out in the spring and strippin' the yellow jasmine . . . And, too, Lord, they're a-tryin' to kill off every God-dogged creature You've got.[23]

Folk attitudes play a major role: the justification of hanging as a suitable penalty for certain criminal acts, the belief that an unmarried girl with child deserved ostracism by the community, and the idea that black people should be relegated to a designated place — one inevitably lower than that of the whites — in the social scale.

Finally, the community's environmental problems quite naturally concern the two institutions of church and school around which life in the hamlet revolves. Almost before the frontier settlers obtain legal grants to their land from the government, the feuding between the Church of Christ and the Baptists starts:

> It was the feud . . . that fanned the spiritual fire in the hearts of the pioneers and gave them zeal to endure hardships and poverty and to work untiringly toward converting the immigrant farmers who poured in a steady stream to the discovered springs.[24]

As the story progresses, the two institutions, so interrelated, become catalysts that hold the people together and engender community spirit. As such, both provide the necessary forces for rivalry and competition upon which the citizens thrive. And if prophet Beene equates the Baptists with the cohorts of the Devil, it enlivens the mainstream of existence in the backwoods village. Besides, it adds piquancy to the communal stew.

The fact that *Joshua Beene And God* is both a compelling satire and folk novel of merit is attributable to its biographic sources. Whether the novelist borrowed directly from seventeenth-century religious folklore in creating Uncle Josh and other characters is conjectural. She does admit, however, that the novel per se is "as true to fact as fiction can get" and that all of her characters are composites of real people she knew.[25] It is possible, then, that in their semi-isolation in the little community and because of their religious fervor, they had retained customs inherited from preceding generations.

For instance, the Baptists, who immigrated to various parts of the South from the Middle Colonies, were originally dissenters of seventeenth-century English Puritanism and, to a great extent, remained Calvinist-oriented. In the late nineteenth century, the denomination still conducted worship services in a manner similar to its Puritan forebears. Consequently, it is logical to think that the church clung to many of the early doctrines and customs and transmitted them to posterity. Indeed, as will be seen, the author's own family tended to reinforce this premise.

Members of the Church of Christ, likewise of frontier origin, while diametrically opposite to the Baptists in some respects, nevertheless had much in common with them. Evolving from the efforts of reform laymen, the church was committed to the restoration of primitive Christianity. Still it adhered to fundamental doctrines, observed the Lord's Supper, preached faith and repentance, and administered baptism as did the Baptists. As a matter of fact, the chief claimant for the archetype of Joshua Beene was a cantankerous and reformist chief elder of the Bald Prairie Church of Christ. The elder, from whom Uncle Josh inherits his physical appearance, protested from his pulpit the custom of young girls riding astride in the neighborhood but insisted that his parishioners pay their just debts.

Born Jewel Henson and the oldest of six daughters, Mrs. Gibson was the product of an austere religious atmosphere. Her parents — J. N. Henson, a stockman and farmer who owned extensive acreage in the community, and Mary Davis Henson, a visionary who wrote a homey novel, *Youth Versus Age,* for the delectation of her adventure-starved neighbors — were staunch Baptists. Mrs. Henson quoted scripture by the hour, and biblical expression frequently punctuated her speech.

Mr. Henson took a pragmatic stance toward the church. A Bible-reading deacon, fundamentalist in doctrine, he believed in paying the preacher to preach and the singing teachers to teach. Both parents agreed on Baptist dogma and ritual, and if they transmitted to their daughter a deep respect for the word of God, they gave her something else. Together, they shaped for her a rigid image of God as a martinet, who enforced His will upon believers as irreversible holy law. When Jewel, as a child, inquired of her mother about the thunder and lightning, Mrs. Henson answered: "Thunder is the voice of the Lord. He taketh the lightning in His hand and centereth the mark." [26] Later, when the author was introduced to Greek mythology, the parallel "Thunder is the voice of Zeus; he holds the thunderbolts in his hands and strikes down his adversaries" had special relevance.

While to the child God was a powerful deity who punished mankind to maintain control over the world, she was aware of the Devil as God's enemy who contended with Him for the domination of it. Just as the Puritans believed that everything originated with God, so did she live in constant fear that God saw everything she did, heard everything she said. She fancied the dead leaves scattered by the wind, as well as the whistling wind itself, as messengers conveying her thoughts and actions to the Almighty.

By the same token, she was frightened of the Devil, whom her parents had described to her as "Old Raw Head and Bloody Bones." To discourage the children from playing around the cistern, one parent hung up an effigy of "Old Raw Head."

This, then, was the rigorous religious environment that spawned the pontifical despot and counterpart of a punitive God, who at the outset of the novel calls upon Him for assistance in subduing the Baptists:

> Fer half a century I've fought the Baptists, and right today there's more Baptists than there was when I begin a-fightin' 'em. Why don't You smite 'em off the face of the earth, Lord?" [27]

Some minutes later, as God commands Josh to look around him, the prophet sees a five-foot moccasin snake on the bank of the creek. To him the snake is symptomatic of the Baptists. Though he smites the reptile with his cane, it escapes into the water. "You're a-goin' to drown him ain't You, Lord? I'll smite 'em, and You'll damn 'em." Then he watches as a pitcher plant lures a fly into its bowl and destroys it. The plant also symbolizes to him the Baptist Church and the fly, the poor unsuspecting sinner stuck within its tentacles with no means of escape. Again Josh smites the plant.

From her earliest years, Mrs. Gibson could recall feuds between the Baptist Church, championed by her parents, and the members of the Church of Christ, sometimes derisively labeled Campbellites in league with Lucifer.

Moreover, the author recalls many instances in the two churches when an elder, or deacon, ordered another member's name dropped from the official denominational roster. The procedure was called unchurching. In Chapter 5, "Of Wine Unsipped And Songs Unsung," crippled Elmer Goolsby, who feels unworthy of partaking of the rite of sacrament, pretends to take part but only raises the wine glass to his lips, without sipping, and permits the unleavened bread to fall to the floor where he guides it to a knothole with his crutch. Although this same procedure has gone on for years seemingly unnoticed, when a Church of Christ member calls Uncle Josh's attention to it, he orders in condemnation, "Scratch him off, Brother Ben."

Other members of the author's family with Puritan tendencies fertilized the well-plowed religious ground in which the novel was rooted. Her Uncle Bill communicated directly with the Lord and, so he claimed, heard the deity's responses. As the story opens, Joshua

Beene commands an audience with God and calls Him down to sit beside him on a log for a conference.

The novelist's maternal grandmother, Mrs. Frances Caroline Davis — an exceedingly strong woman, half-Cajun and half-English — influenced her formative years. Mrs. Davis's Puritan legacy was the curse. Because of a series of disasters (her husband had been murdered, a son had died accidentally by an "empty gun," and a granddaughter had been the victim of a domestic tragedy), Mrs. Davis was convinced that God had called down a curse upon her house. As a result she regaled young Jewel almost unceasingly with gruesome accounts of the catastrophes. In Chapter 3, Joshua pronounces a curse on Leonard Johnson — a power he ostensibly heired from the flamboyant grandam with a pronounced Cajun accent straight out of the Louisiana Bayou Teche country.

An integral part of the community's religious life that left its impact on *Joshua Beene And God* was the annual summer revival, or protracted meeting, usually held under a brush arbor such as Mrs. Gibson depicts in the so-called Holy Roller service in Chapter 4. The revival, an event enthusiastically supported in the community, was to the dispirited, back-slidden Baptist what a highly publicized tonic is said to be to people of today with rundown, "iron poor blood." At such gatherings rededication was a way of life. When a person failed the Lord it was necessary to atone, and atonement was invariably accompanied by a renewal of faith or a rededication. Thus, it was obvious that Uncle Josh, upon realizing that he has not measured up to God's expectations on his sixty-ninth birthday, would rededicate himself to the task. In the first chapter, when the Lord inquires if Josh is satisfied, he answers:

> Jist forgive me, Lord. I'm more than satisfied, and I'm a-renewin' my pledge with You right now. I ain't got but one more year down here on this sin-infested earth, but I'll guarantee You one thing: when my time is up, there won't be enough Baptists left at Spring Creek fer You to shoot a star at.[28]

Mrs. Gibson was baptized in the muddy waters of Duck Creek at the age of eleven. By her fourteenth birthday, she had rededicated herself — this time as a missionary to the heathens in Africa. Also by this time, she had begun to develop a protective role for others that belied her years. As the oldest of six siblings, she supervised her younger sisters and looked after their interests at school and elsewhere. This experience of directing others later developed into a feeling of responsibility that remained a permanent characteristic.

Before her seventeenth birthday, the author married Felix Gibson, a driller of oil wells, who convinced her that she could fulfill her missionary commitment by helping people at home instead of going to Africa. Her husband encouraged her to finish high school, which the marriage had interrupted, and gave her a university education to prepare her for a third dedication — that of instructing Texas schoolchildren.

The characterization of Joshua Beene thus expanded into a projection of Jewel Gibson herself. It was but a natural transfer for the novelist to invest the messiah of Spring Creek not only with her early religious concepts and her knowledge of the scriptures worthy of a serious theologian, but also with the sense of paternalism for the sinners of Spring Creek, her own feelings of responsibility for others functioning in the opposite gender.

The civic environment in which Jewel Henson matured — one in which moral precepts were both instilled by word of mouth and demonstrated by example — also had a notable effect on the novel. Mr. Henson, a profoundly moral man, was dedicated to maintaining the sanctity of the home. He believed that an honorable man was justified in taking a life to protect his family. Such deep-rooted moral philosophy fomented radicalism. It also led men to rationalize mob action and the taking of the law into their own hands.

In Chapter 2, "The Mob Strikes," Uncle Josh at the age of seven recalls his first experience in relating to a mob. He had remembered hearing his mother plead with his father: "Give him a fair trial, Ebenezer. Get you a jury and try the man. Give him a chance." He also recalls his father's answer: "He's one that ain't deserving of a chance, Sarah." The next morning little Joshua listens with filial admiration as his father describes the details of the incident.

Here again Mrs. Gibson dips into the family album. She had heard her own mother plead with her father not to join a mob to storm the Franklin jail and hang the man who had brutally murdered his wife.

Then, at seventeen, Uncle Josh is inducted into the "fraternity" when he leads a mob to avenge the death of his father. Later he would try to justify the custom: "Hanging didn't show animosity. It showed respect for principle." [29]

Closely related to the casual approach to mob action and violence is the intense racism that prevailed in the South during the immediate post-Civil War period and persisted for some years in remote areas. Thus, just as the novelist's father struggled with his own conscience over race prejudice, so does Joshua Beene in the novel. In his first confrontation with God, he says: "You ain't no respector of persons are You, Lord? Do race or color have any influence with You?" To which God replies that Joshua could read and must answer the question for himself.

Still the Spring Creek prophet vacillates. At the opening of Chapter 2, "Of Effigies and Robes Unspotted," after Joshua has completed his plan to prevent the expulsion of the mulatto boy by the Baptist schoolboard members, he tells himself that "he had not the least enthusiasm for racial justice. No man could call him a nigger-lover, for he believed in everyone's keeping his designated place." However, by the end of the chapter, Uncle Josh has mellowed sufficiently to reverse himself. The night after Leonard Johnson had aroused the mob which raised the effigy on the flagpole — an act no doubt motivated by the incident of "Old Raw Head" at the cistern — the prophet of Spring Creek removes Volume J from his shelves and mutters "Nigger hater" to himself as he records an observation: "It's possible for men to become so white that they're leprous."

At this crucial point the contest is no longer one to determine whether a Baptist or a member of the Church of Christ will deliver the valedictory at the high school commencement. It has mushroomed into an ugly racial struggle for which men would resort once more to the noose as a leveler. But Uncle Josh has undergone a spiritual catharsis even as Jewel Gibson had recovered from her earlier disquieting concept of a deity of chastisement. Once more she interjects personal experience into her story as Uncle Josh saves the life of the boy of mixed blood, Wain McIvory, and "splints the wings of the fallen sparrow" — Pearl Gaston.

This is a prelude to the final scene in Chapter 15, "The Prophecy Is Fulfilled," in which Joshua Beene redeems the sinners of Spring Creek from their astronomical fear and ignorance and frees the Baptists from their colossal bigotry. No longer is he the tyrannical prophet of Spring Creek striking terror into the hearts of his charges. His metamorphosis is complete. Deified, Joshua Beene keeps his appointment with God.

Two questions invariably surface about *Joshua Beene And God*. Why did Mrs. Gibson write the novel and why did it take her so long? The second question merits scrutiny first. Since she admits having started in 1930 and did not complete the novel — that is, offer the manuscript for publication — until 1945, it was assumed that she devoted fifteen years to the project. In fact, one Texas editor made this amazing observation: "But it's just as well that Mrs. Gibson took fifteen years to write *Joshua Beene And God*. Just as well, too, that early this year she became eligible for retirement from public school teaching for chances are she'd have been retired anyway." [30] The editor was correct in only one respect. Mrs. Gibson had met the retirement condition for Texas public schoolteachers, but she had no intention of retiring at forty. Moreover, although there had been talk of asking Mrs. Gibson to resign because of the book, she had already advanced to a better position.

The fact remained, however, that she did not devote fifteen years to the actual writing of *Joshua Beene And God*. As early as 1930, the author toyed with the idea of doing such a novel and began to jot down notes. In 1930 she had taught high school speech and English for only three years and was engrossed in her career, which was exceedingly time-consuming with extracurricular chores claiming her attention before and after her teaching schedule began. But by the time the novel was submitted to a publisher, she had taught eighteen years. Actually, Mrs. Gibson wrote the first draft in six or eight weeks.

Why did Mrs. Gibson write the novel? Reasons date back to the author's childhood. It was like an experiment for which one cannot tabulate his findings until he has verified the results. What *Joshua Beene And God* is basically all about, stripped of its fictional trappings, is one woman's search for God. The child of partisan Baptist parents, Mrs. Gibson identified God as a martinet struggling for control of the world — her mother's God of thunder and lightning, her father's God of fundamentalism. Only a few years later, perhaps after she had started to public school, whether she was conscious of it or not, the sensitive little girl rejected the God of lightning and thunder, the God of fundamental doctrine, to embark on her own lonely pilgrimage.

Since she had been taught that God created the flowers and birds and animals and since she loved them, despite an earlier fear, she turned first in her search to nature. But at the outset neither did the God she sought in nature bring her peace.

Mrs. Gibson remembers the first time she watched with enchantment as a spider wove its silken web. But her enchantment was ephemeral. When an insect ensnared itself in the web, the weaver injected it with juices and sucked the liquified remains into its mouth — to the observing child's horror. Another time she saw a male spider approach a female, the larger of the species, gingerly before engaging in copulation lest she eat him. Ironically, after the mating act, the male was not quick enough to escape. She also remembers the time she became terrorized when she witnessed a snake charm a defenseless sparrow and swallow it whole, and she was powerless to save it.[31]

She continued her search — this time through daily reading of the Bible. Clergymen and her parents alike encouraged her with the reassurance that all of her questions would be answered, all mysteries cleared away. Although she gained a storehouse of religious information, the God she was seeking still eluded her. The biblical God of the four Gospels was a magnificent creature — a subject to challenge the skill and imagination of artists throughout the ages. But to the curious child He remained aloof. He remained intangible, an idea, a story figure — unreal.

It was consoling to recall that the character Pilgrim from her favorite book did not attain his destination of the Celestial City overnight or without facing obstacles along the way. Still almost in desperation, in her early teens, she considered transferring her quest to a foreign country, where among lowly people of a different ethnic group she might find God. Meanwhile, she married and continued her search at home.

So the search went on. Though Mrs. Gibson never lost faith, she wondered at times if she were worthy of the quest. Galahad's quest for the Holy Grail had been rewarded because he, alone of the three searchers, had been worthy. Finally, after many more years of seeking, Jewel Gibson found God. She did not find Him in the crowded streets of the city, with its inevitable brothels, crime syndicates, and corrupt politicians. Jewel Gibson found God in the small towns where she taught. She found God among underprivileged youth — society's pawns, ill-clad, neglected, and often in revolt against life's harsh realities. She found God among young people seeking escape like Huck Finn, who with the aid of a noble black man discovered his God in the shape of a river. Huck's God was a deity of liberation freeing him from the bonds of racial intolerance, the enslavement of ignorance, the whiplash of fear. Jewel Gibson's was a God of love.

Huck Finn has held his undisputed place as the all-American boy for ninety-four years. As America approaches its tercentenary, Joshua Beene occupies his own special niche in belletristic letters — no longer contested and indestructible.

Patsy Woodall: Huntsville Legend

For over half a century, despite hurricanes and other acts of God, she printed the *Huntsville Item* without missing a single issue. Almost any day you are likely to meet the blue-eyed, statuesque blonde behind the wheel of her car at a Huntsville supermarket, picking up groceries, or at one of the town's banks, attending to business.

The ubiquitous woman is Mrs. Ross Woodall, the town's beloved Miss Patsy and Huntsville legend. On May 29, 1984, the perennially *young* lady reached her ninety-fourth milestone.

Former owner and publisher of the *Huntsville Item*, the state's second oldest newspaper, Miss Patsy and the Woodall family piloted its course for over fifty-three years. Ross Woodall, Jr., succeeded his father, who died in 1943, and served with his mother as copublisher until his death in 1957. In 1967 Harte-Hanks Communications, Inc., a newspaper chain based in San Antonio, purchased the 134-year-old newspaper, second in age only to the *Dallas Morning News*.

Miss Patsy maintains a close relationship with the present *Item* staff. In fact, her daughter-in-law, Nelda Woodall, a columnist for the publication, is a link between the past and the present. Terry

29

Scott Bertling, present editor, holds the former publisher up as a role model.

"Miss Patsy means a lot to the *Item*," Bertling said. "She and her commitment to good newspapering and to making her community a better place to live serve as a model for the rest of us."

The *Item* marked Miss Patsy's ninety-fourth anniversary with a reception. Highlight of the celebration was the unveiling of oil portraits of Miss Patsy and former longtime editor, the late Don Reid, accompanied by citations for their outstanding contributions to the paper's twentieth-century progress. The portraits will hang permanently in the foyer of the newspaper quarters located at the corner of 19th Street and Avenue H.

Miss Patsy grew up in a rural environment. The third of eight children, she was born in the East Texas community of White-wright in Grayson County and moved with her family to Alvin when she was two. William Byron Finger and his wife Emma, her parents, settled their family on acreage in the Mustang community five miles from Alvin.

As was customary, the children performed chores on the farm. Patsy's main contribution to the family dairy enterprise was to milk seven cows twice daily. So it was with a milkmaid's stool and a three-gallon bucket that she faced the world each morning at 5:00. After finishing, she mounted her favorite gray mare and drove the animals to pasture. At 5:00 in the evening, after returning from school, she retrieved them and repeated the chore.

When the males in the family had an emergency in the hay fields, Patsy milked as many as thirty cows — half of the herd. Familiar with the techniques of harvesting and baling hay, she also helped out in the fields when necessary.

While her two sisters busied themselves with housework, Patsy teamed with her brother Marvin, two years older than she, on outside chores. In addition to the milking, the two were adept with a saw and hammer in making minor repairs on the farm property. Patsy hardly realized her gender until she was twelve or thirteen and received instruction in the feminine crafts of cooking and sewing.

Patsy Finger got her introduction to Huntsville in 1910, when she enrolled in the Sam Houston Normal Institute to qualify for a teaching certificate. Boardinghouses provided living quarters for the students at the time, and Patsy secured lodging at the home of Mrs. S. M. Elkins one block from the campus. The Elkins house accommodated twelve young ladies, and its advertisements stressed that "telephone service, electric lights, and hot and cold baths [were] among the comforts provided."

Mrs. Elkins was the mother of James A. Elkins, who later became known as Judge Elkins — a holdover from his law practice — and the financier who developed Elkins Lake Estates in Huntsville and founded First City National Bank in Houston.

Jim, as his friends called him, was a hero to the farm girl from Alvin. Even in his earlier years, Elkins had the Midas touch. "He literally lived and breathed money," she said. Elkins told Patsy Finger that anything was possible if a person just put his mind to it.

Later, after he became a power in the economy of Houston and the biggest banker in the Southwest, Elkins tried to interest Patsy Woodall in a chain of newspapers, but she felt that the *Huntsville Item* was enough to handle.

Miss Patsy met Ross Woodall at Sam Houston before she was graduated in 1912. The couple fell in love, but Patsy taught school briefly before they were married, to repay a loan she had made to finance her education. The Woodalls married in 1914 and returned to Huntsville to put down permanent roots.

Huntsville was scarcely more than a village when Miss Patsy first discovered it. The square centered by the courthouse was the hub around which activity revolved — the rectangle watered by Pleasant Gray's springs, with its intersections identified as Barrett's, Foster's, Gibb's, and Smither's corners. Miss Patsy recalls the board sidewalks with hitching posts attached and the unpaved streets so muddy during the rainy season that some vehicles got mired to the axles.

Wagons, some equipped with two seats, were the chief means of transportation. A few sons of well-to-do families drove flashy buggies behind blooded horseflesh. Few families had four-wheeled carriages and buckboard surreys. Miss Patsy recalls when only such solid citizens as the Gibbses, the Smithers, and the McKinneys had the more luxurious means of conveyance. There were livery stables, from which you could rent a mount, if you were lucky, or hire a hack.

She can remember when the town, outside of the square and

the normal institute and prison, consisted only of such reference points as the old water tank and Tilley's Tap, the eight-mile spur railroad from Huntsville to Phelps. Tilley operated the train to suit himself, she said, often taking time out on a run to fish in a convenient pond while his passengers waited. He could be accommodating, however, occasionally delaying his schedule for the convenience of late passengers.

At least once Tilley played the role of hero. That was when escaped convicts commandeered his train to escape to Phelps and make contact with the main I&GN line. Tilley moved the train so slowly that the sheriff and his posse were waiting for his arrival at Phelps.

Miss Patsy marvels at the town's evolution since those early days. But Huntsville's greatest change, she said, has been in the people.

"People in Huntsville are less clannish, less class-conscious than they were during the century's infancy. They gradually moved away from the old binding mores of Southern regionalism. Today they are cosmopolitan and more unified in civic affairs."

In the half century that Miss Patsy and her family published the *Item*, the paper became a moulder of public opinion and a political barometer of the Walker County area. It was, as well, the voice of the historical community where Huntsville's most illustrious native son, the author-artist-Marine John W. Thomason, and Texas heroes Sam Houston and Henderson Yoakum were buried.

More important, the *Item* became a vital force in the building of modern Huntsville. Of the civic achievements championed by the paper, Miss Patsy's favorite is the Huntsville Memorial Hospital. The facility was erected originally in 1927 as a monument to Huntsville youth who fell in World War I.

A breakthrough came in 1926 when Ella Smither donated her home on Avenue O to the city for conversion into a hospital. When the Woodalls saw the papers certifying the gift, they knew that the *Item* had won a battle.

On April 4, 1927, the hospital was chartered as a nonprofit corporation for the use of all citizens of Huntsville regardless of race. The first board of trustees included the following officers: R. W. Miller, chairman; J. E. Allen, vice-chairman; Tom Ball, treasurer; and E. C. Boynton, secretary. Other members were H. F. Estill, J. L. Pritchett, W. T. Robinson, C. N. Shaver, and T. E. Humphrey. The corporation was responsible for maintenance, support, and operation. By March 10, 1927, two-thirds of the funds necessary to remodel the Smither property were raised. The one-story building with a patient capacity of sixteen to eighteen that resulted was an inauspicious beginning.

With additions made as needed, this structure served the community until September 24, 1950, when it was replaced by a brick building with a fifty-bed capacity.

Throughout the years, the hospital remained one of Miss Patsy's primary interests. She was instrumental in organizing the Huntsville Memorial Hospital Auxiliary. In conjunction with the organization, she established a snack bar at the facility and was its sole operator for several years. Later, as the project caught on, she employed two assistants. At the outset, Miss Patsy not only prepared and served the food, she financed the project. After the snack bar became cost-effective, Miss Patsy estimates in the fourteen years of its operation it yielded $75,000 in profits that provided equipment for the hospital.

When the project was discontinued and an arts and crafts gift shop was installed, Miss Patsy was one of its most enthusiastic supporters. Frequently, she entertains members of the auxiliary in her home and directs the arts and crafts activities.

Miss Patsy's involvement with the hospital was not without its tense moments. Once when there were no doctors present and only one nurse on duty, she ministered at the birth of an infant. The nurse rushed up to Miss Patsy. "Come quickly," she said. "Two women in the ward are giving birth."

"But I've never . . . ," protested Miss Patsy.

"Hurry," the nurse interrupted, pushing Miss Patsy into the room. "You take that one and I'll take this one."

A doctor returned in time to observe Miss Patsy spanking the newborn into life. He took the neonate from her. "I didn't know you were versed in midwifery," he said.

Miss Patsy hoped her nervousness was not showing. "You can't be expected to know everything, doctor," she quipped.

One other time Miss Patsy was pressed into medical service. Because of a mixup in communications, a doctor was faced with setting a man's broken leg — a really bad injury — with no anesthe-tist on hand.

When Miss Patsy hesitated, the surgeon assured her that she could do what he told her to do. She did.

Throughout the sixties, improvements and additions to the hospital were made to meet the increasing needs of the community. Then, with the advent of the seventies, the growth of Huntsville was such that the abandonment of the old building was recom-mended with a replacement to be made at a different location. The board of trustees decided to establish a hospital district, but the proposal resulted in a division of public opinion. In two referen-dums, one held November 2, 1971, and another, February 14, 1972, the citizens of Huntsville defeated the issue.

Since her husband's death in 1943, Miss Patsy had been at the paper's helm. Again she realized she had a job to do, and she was determined to succeed. The *Item* had to reverse the views of con-servative Huntsville on the need for a modern hospital district. The year 1973 came and went without incident. They called it the Bat-tle for the Certificate of Need Year, a battle that failed. But Miss Patsy kept plugging away.

Finally, on November 4, 1975, the voters of Walker County registered their approval of the Walker County Hospital District. On November 18, 1976, the Walker County District signed a con-tract for the construction of the facility at a cost of over $12 million.

Groundbreaking ceremonies were held on September 1, 1977, for the hospital district to be located at 3000 Interstate 45. Miss Patsy turned the first spadeful of dirt. The implement was pre-sented to her after the ceremonies and remains one of the most treasured trophies highlighting her long career. Today that shovel, elegantly gilded with gold leaf, occupies a conspicuous space on her living room wall displaying her mementos and trophies.

The hospital, consisting of 134,000 square feet of floor space with a bed capacity of 144, is staffed by a team of doctors and sur-geons of national reputation in their respective disciplines. The fa-cility is maintained by Hospital Corporation of America, a publicly owned health care company which owns and/or manages a net-work of more than 400 hospitals throughout the nation and abroad.

In the foyer of the hospital proper is a gold-lettered plaque tes-tifying to the dedicated service Patsy Woodall rendered the institu-tion:

"Miss Patsy" Woodall
in Recognition of Distinguished and
Dedicated Service as Founding Member
Walker County Hospital District
1975–1979

But the newspaperwoman's impact was not limited to the parameters of Huntsville and Walker County. Prominently involved with the Associated Press, Miss Patsy helped to found Texas Gulf Coast Press Association in 1939. She headed the organization as president in 1954–55 and is still an active member.

For years, Miss Patsy was a leader in the Democratic Party of Texas. As a public relations woman with her own newspaper as outlet, she developed a special interest in government and in politicians who make it function. Moreover, as senatorial committeewoman for six years and member of the board of the Texas Press Association, she had audience privileges with the Senate in session. She helped to elect three governors of Texas and served as state publicity director for Franklin Delano Roosevelt's fourth campaign for the presidency in 1944, with headquarters at the Adolphus Hotel in Dallas.

The governors were Ross Sterling (1931–1933), Allan Shivers (1949–1957), and Price Daniel, Sr. (1957–1963). The Woodalls and Sterlings became close friends and exchanged visits.

"Sterling was a generous man," she said. "It was during the depression, and many of us were biting the bullet then. It was the state's loss that Mrs. Ferguson defeated us the second time around."

Both Shivers and Daniel were worthy public servants, she said, but she was partial to Shivers, an East Texan with a background similar to her own. As lieutenant governor during Beauford Jester's administration, Shivers completed the governor's unexpired term when Jester died suddenly on July 11, 1940. He then went on to serve a total of seven and a half years.

"Shivers was controversial," she said, "but powerful. He ruffled some feathers when he switched to the Republican party and carried the state for General Eisenhower in the presidential election of 1952. They called him Shivercrat in derision."

It had not been easy to get Roosevelt reelected for his fourth term. "Ambition destroyed Roosevelt," she said. "In spite of all of

his accomplishments, he was too sick, both physically and men-
tally, to run for a fourth term."

She considered Eleanor Roosevelt a greater person than the
president. "Eleanor said that Roosevelt had a dialogue with the
American people. Eleanor Roosevelt had a dialogue with the
world."

President Roosevelt offered Miss Patsy a job on his staff in
Washington, but her roots in Huntsville were too deep to abandon.
Then he died of a cerebral hemorrhage on April 12, 1945.

Miss Patsy thought Truman was an interesting man but less
than outstanding as a chief executive. She declined to work for Lyndon Johnson because of his unsavory reputation. "It was not surprising," she said, "that Vietnam destroyed him." She felt that
Ford was a man of poor judgment who probably increased in stature after he left the Oval Office. She believed John F. Kennedy was
destined for greatness had his assassin not cut him down.

Nixon? "He was not strong enough to resist temptation."
Carter? "A good man but definitely not of presidential timber."

A gourmet cook, Miss Patsy maintains a place at Sunset Lake,
where she enjoys entertaining. Nor is she an amateur on the sport-
ing end of a cane fishing pole. Many are the afternoons she's
yanked enough perch and bass out of the lake, which her rear deck
overlooks, in time to prepare a delicious fish dinner for family and
friends. Although abstemious herself, she can also double at the
bar, her specialties being Margaritas and rum colas.

Despite her time-consuming professional life, Miss Patsy succeeded in rearing an interesting family. Her late son was a community leader and enthusiastic sportsman as well as newspaperman. He was among the first young men in Huntsville to enlist for
duty in World War II, serving in the Air Force.

Miss Patsy's daughters, Bess (Mrs. Frank Murray) of Huntsville and Glen Woodall Karsten of Houston, followed in their
mother's footsteps. When World War II reduced the manpower on
the paper staff to one disabled employee, the daughters insisted
upon working full time with their mother. Glen assumed the editor-
ship and became proficient at setting copy on the linotype. Bess,
who resigned her teaching job at Flatonia, learned to operate the
cylinder press and the folder. In fact, the shorthanded staff mas-

tered all the skills necessary to get the paper out and fill job printing orders.

"It was a tremendous amount of work," Miss Patsy said. "The *Item* would not have survived if each of us hadn't pitched in to do the work of two or three."

Today Mrs. Murray, wife of a Huntsville businessman, is a teacher at the Texas Department of Corrections. Her teaching career spans three decades.

Widow of the late Texas oilman Floyd L. Karsten, Jr., Glen founded the Living Bank International in 1968, with headquarters at Texas Medical Center in Houston. The Living Bank coordinates the referral of human organ donations pledged before death to the appropriate medical facilities for transplantation, therapy, and medical research. Persons from all fifty states and sixty foreign countries are members of the organization. Endowed by the Floyd L. Karsten, Jr. Foundation, the nonprofit organization receives no financial support from United Way or from federal agencies.

As founding president, Mrs. Karsten heads the Living Bank, assisted by a board of directors and a board of advisers. Miss Patsy is a member of the board of advisers and an ardent supporter of her daughter's work. Among those serving with Miss Patsy are the Houston cardiovascular surgeons Dr. Denton A. Cooley and Dr. Michael E. DeBakey, the noted Dr. Christiaan N. Barnard of Capetown, South Africa, Vice-President George Bush, motion picture personalities Roy Rogers and Dale Evans, and columnist Abigail Van Buren.

Miss Patsy has five grandchildren and four great-grandchildren and an adorable poodle named Christina, all of whom she spoils outrageously. The family is close-knit and gets together often. Christmas is a big event in the Woodall family tradition, when all of the clan assemble at Miss Patsy's lake place, which includes a guest house in addition to the main cottage. Miss Patsy decorates the cottages for Christmas with ornaments she creates from discarded costume jewelry and other colorful gewgaws. She has developed these decorating skills into such a fine art that Christmas around Huntsville isn't complete until you've seen and experienced the magic of Miss Patsy's winter wonderland.

For the most part, Miss Patsy's gifts are also handmade — things she has knitted like afghans, socks, sweaters, and capes.

World-traveled, Miss Patsy still receives mail from foreign ad-
mirers. Not long ago a postman rang her doorbell persistently.

"Letter for you, Miss Patsy," he said. "Got a foreign stamp on
it. Might be important."

The letter was postmarked Paris, France. The brief super-
scription read: "To the Queen of Huntsville, Texas, U.S.A."

Monte Barrett and the Writing Trade

A forthright influence on my writing career at the outset was Monte Barrett, author of popular *Saturday Evening Post* serials and best-selling novels.

I had introduced two new courses to the Sam Houston State College campus in 1947 — creative writing and Literature of the Southwest — and President Harmon Lowman and George Evans, head of the English Department, decided that it would be in my interest and that of my students for me to attend the Writers Conference sponsored by the University of Oklahoma at Norman in the summer of 1949.

Stanley Vestal (also known on the campus as Professor Walter S. Campbell) and Foster Harris, who had established one of the most successful professional writing schools in the nation, would be in charge of the Writers Conference. The three-day affair was an annual event that served as a highlight of the Oklahoma University writing courses.

I had a healthy respect for Vestal's writing texts and books dealing with the West and Southwest. So when I was given the opportunity to attend the conference with expenses subsidized by the

college, I graciously accepted. It was at this time that I met Monte
Barrett and J. Evetts Haley.

My most sustained achievement, aside from newspaper features and published poems, was a creative project — a 500-line,
blank-verse poem — submitted as a partial requirement for the
master of arts degree conferred by The University of Texas, in lieu
of a thesis, in 1945. I learned a great deal from Barrett, whose novels based on Texas history I had recommended to my students enrolled in Literature of the Southwest. He was most generous in
sharing the fruits of his rich experience with beginners like myself.
Much of the advice he gave and many of the writing techniques he
discussed I was able to appropriate for my own use and transfer to
my students with remarkable success. Barrett did not address his
remarks to potential novelists exclusively but gave specific advice
and practicable ideas in general about writing as a craft.

To the San Antonio author, writing was definitely a trade — a
trade whose fundamental tools were sincerity and hard work. Certainly, he dispelled any illusions one may have had about the
profession.

I can see him now, center stage, holding a hand microphone
that never worked for him and with which he gestured, aware that
it was dead. "The long-hair in his velvet gown seated in a bay window waiting for the lightning to strike" was a figment of the imagination, according to Monte Barrett.

To begin with, then, to the budding young literary aspirant,
Barrett proposed, "Learn your trade; be a craftsman." Convinced
that it was just as important for a successful writer to master the
tools of his trade as it was for a doctor to acquire essential skills of
medicine and surgery or a lawyer, necessary legal procedure, the
author, self-effacingly modest, declared: "I have sincerity, and I
hope someday I may be a craftsman too."

For examples of real craftsmen, or writers who had mastered
the tools of the writing trade, Barrett cited two, who in his opinion,
were at the top: John P. Marquand, creator of Mr. Moto, and Ben
Ames Williams, author of the lengthy *House Divided*. Neither of
these had any illusions about writing but earned his place through
persistent industry, the novelist declared.

As to style, the beginner simply needs to keep his feet on the
ground, Barrett advised. "The minute the reader thinks you have

consciously tried to write beautifully, you cease to be impressive," he said. "In fact, the story is interrupted. That's bad."

With no small irony, Barrett told the following anecdote. An effusive lady at an autographing party gushed to him, a young man-of-letters reveling in the plaudits of an early success in 1920: "I just adore your book, Mr. Barrett, and," looking up kittenishly into his eyes, "I found the hidden meaning in the final paragraph on page 179."

"The hidden meaning!" young author Barrett uttered, flabbergasted. Hell, he said, he'd hoped there wasn't any hidden meaning.

During the twenties and thirties, some writers intent upon developing individual style held up Ernest Hemingway as a prototype. Barrett's answer to this was that the way Hemingway wrote was natural for Hemingway, and any attempt to imitate him would only result in affectation, which — to say the least — was unpleasant. All style *is*, he insisted, is good writing; and good writing is sincere writing. Asked to elaborate, Barrett defined style as "the natural growth of expression within yourself, of which you — the writer — are unconscious."

To illustrate, he told of some writing on which he seemed to be stymied until his understanding publisher came forth with: "I scared you with style while you were with book." Barrett recalled that he literally wore out a thesaurus when he first began to write, whereas later he rarely consulted one, having long since learned that the simple, familiar word is best.

"All fancy-pants words are out," he insisted. "If you send your reader to the dictionary, you have interrupted the flow of your story."

Monte Barrett served the usual apprenticeship of the man with a newspaper background. From cub reporter he advanced to managing editor, covering a couple of wars on the way (he was in the navy during World War I) — all without regret. Accordingly, he had seen most of the angles of the profession from the practical side. Besides this, his experience since his retirement from newspaper work in 1928 had been relatively varied. He had written his first newspaper serial back in 1921. He explored the pulp field before it declined, then progressed rapidly to the slicks. He had affixed his byline to mystery stories and to historical fiction, all in addition to his acclaimed serials.

In 1927 he created the syndicated comic strip *Jane Arden*, on which he collaborated with Russell Ross. He also had had his own radio show based on the comic series. Before World War II, he was under contract to Warner Brothers of Hollywood; thus he had crowded screenwriting into his heterogeneous experience. No doubt about it, Barrett had paid his union dues.

How did the novelist write? "I write every way" was his answer. Some writers protest that dictating slows down productivity or that they can't think without coordinating their minds with finger movement at the typewriter keyboard. Such was not the case with Monte Barrett. He could either pick it out on two fingers himself if he had to or dictate with fluency. In fact, he rather preferred dictating copy for the reason that it helped him to revise. Fresh copy carefully done by another person was to this author like new manuscript in which revision went much faster.

Barrett attributed his knowledge of dictation to the war. Standard equipment for his job, he explained, "included a good secretary, and I just naturally learned to use her. Why let her go to waste?"

As to the novelist's specific method, how he wrote *Smoke Up the Valley* (1949) was a case in point. *Post* editors had liked *Tempered Blade* (1946) but had rejected *Sun In Their Eyes* (1944) because of excessive length. Nevertheless, they contracted with him for a forthcoming serial and he got started on it.

With the first chapter out of the typewriter, the story seemed to be going well. But something happened meanwhile, and by the time he was in the middle of the last chapter (which was on a Thursday afternoon) he stopped abruptly and told his secretary to go home and not to return until the following Monday. When she returned on Monday he did not finish the final chapter. Instead he spent two days dictating to himself everything that was wrong with the story. He had tried so hard to please the *Post* editors that he had sacrificed integrity. Consequently, he had the secretary take a letter in which he informed the *Post* that he could not write the serial as they wanted; in short, the deal was off. This first version of *Smoke Up the Valley* ran to 60,000 words.

Then Barrett rewrote the story in the form of a novel. Barrett explained that there is a great deal of difference between the writing techniques of a serial and a novel. For one thing, you have more latitude in the novel and the serial must be considerably tighter. The novel ran to 185,000 words. It was a completely new job, even the heroine differing from that of the serial. The serial had begun when the protagonist was thirteen. In the novel, the story began when the protagonist was twenty-four. The author had changed the arbitrary beginning for his introduction. The *Post* saw this and liked it.

After further conferences with his editors, the indefatigable Barrett did still a third version of the yarn. The work had to be cut mercilessly, but fortunately the writer was satisfied that it was for the improvement of the material as well as for the reduction of length. Acting upon one editor's suggestion, he returned to his original beginning as of the first serial. Next, he set to work diligently pulling out threads. A different set of characters thus began to emerge, while others were deleted. The plot had to be adjusted to the character changes. Within six weeks, however, the novelist had the third version of *Smoke Up the Valley*, a serial this time of which he himself approved, all set to go. He had completed a tremendous revision job and had cut his wordage from 185,000 to approximately 65,000. The *Post* prefers serials somewhat shorter. They published *Smoke Up the Valley* in this new version under the title of *Rustler's Range*. The three versions of the story had required the better part of two years, the average time many writers take for one book.

Blue-eyed, balding, and portly, with no indication of paunchiness, Monte Barrett, at the half-century mark or a year or two beyond, could well afford to have sat back and rested on his laurels. Royalties from any one of his three books involving Texas history — *Tempered Blade, Sun In Their Eyes, Smoke Up the Valley* — would have been adequate for retirement, not to mention dividends from Jane Arden and from the sale of the twenty-five-cent pocket editions of his works, one of which had been issued in five languages. But pragmatist that he was, he went right on maintaining a consistent daily working schedule, sometimes averaging 5,000 words a day when in the middle of a story.

Whereas some writers grind out 1,000 words of finished copy for an average four-hour stint, Barrett worked for a longer period and insisted he never turned out finished copy. His explanation: "I keep plugging at it, trying to revise it and smooth it out. This happens more than once. There'd be no way for me to tell how much copy I turned out in a given period, speaking quite frankly, because the revision continues over a long time. I think when I'm in the middle of a story, I probably average four to five thousand words a day, but this is not finished copy. Also, this figure would vary." There were times when he turned out as little as 1,000 words a day.

Barrett kept Jane Arden strips on file four months in advance and admitted that he alternated between a current novel and the comic series. That is to say, he could be working on a novel and the comic series simultaneously without loss of time or subsequent confusion.

Although the author believed it unwise for a writer to drive himself beyond his native capacity, Barrett retained a newspaperman's respect for a deadline. Moreover, he had learned from experience. Once he was faced by the dilemma of producing 60,000 words in a day and a half. "We've run your first installment," an editor reminded Barrett. "Now where's the rest of the story?" Where was it indeed? The positive answer then was a pressing matter also for economic reasons, the lush years of Barrett still being in the distant future. The editor got his copy.

But the novelist realized the necessity for relaxation. A part of his routine was to spend an hour loafing in his garden at his San Antonio home after a grueling stint at the typewriter or a long dictating session with his secretary.

Unlike some men whose appearance belied their profession, the genial, comfortably dressed Monte Barrett, almost six feet without shoes, and distinguished by a meticulously trimmed mustache on his upper lip, looked like an author. You felt, even as you first met him, that such a man could do nothing but write. It may have been the way he stood, relaxed and unposed, usually with one hand thrust deep into a pocket and the other gesturing, sometimes wildly with his cane, which he always carried. It most assuredly had something to do with the intensity of his expression when he talked to you.

You rarely hear the name of Monte Barrett today. But when I learned of his death in New York in October 1949, scarcely four months after the Writers Conference, I knew how fortunate I had been. Now, more than three decades later, I recognize my indebtedness to Monte Barrett.

Riding the Trail with
J. Evetts Haley

Before I met J. Evetts Haley at the Writers Conference in Norman, Oklahoma, in 1949, I had read his six books, including his latest, *Jeff Milton: A Good Man with a Gun* (1948). I had incorporated into my course Literature of the Southwest material from his first book, *The XIT Ranch of Texas and the Early Days of the Llano Estacado*, which had been withdrawn soon after its publication in 1929 because of ensuing litigation.[1]

I still recall with mixed emotions an incident relating to the latter. Sam Houston State University Library had two copies of *The XIT Ranch of Texas*, despite the fact that it had been suppressed.[2] As I was planning my course, I prevailed upon a librarian to permit me to check out one of the copies to study over the weekend. The rare book was valued at upwards of $1,000, and it was against the regulations to remove it from the library. But I was pressed for time and needed to integrate the material into my syllabus before the new semester began.

Fortunately, I work relatively fast and had finished my study on Saturday afternoon. When the head of the library staff learned on Sunday that I had one of the rare copies at my apartment at Country Campus, he rushed out to retrieve it. Since I was a member of the faculty and trustworthy, I felt his anxiety was misplaced. I informed him that I had intended to return the book by Monday morning early and doubted that I had deprived anyone of the privilege of browsing it, meanwhile, in the Texas Room, where the rare books and Southwestern collections were shelved.

That was not what worried him. The tar-paper shacks at Country Campus were like tinderboxes. My place could have caught fire in the interim and destroyed the rare book! Thus my psychological approach to J. Evetts Haley, two years before I had had the pleasure of meeting him in the flesh, had not been without its theatrics.

The incident whetted my desire to meet the man who at twenty-eight could write a book that would incite legal action — a volume in my own university library valued at $1,000. Twenty years had elapsed since the book was published, and the author, whose name had become a household word, would be in his late forties.

What was the Haley of 1949 vintage like? A singularly handsome man — oval-faced, sun-tanned, and with twinkling eyes as blue as indigo — Haley appeared to be much younger than his forty-eight years. Women hung on his every word, positively drooled over him. Nor was I immune. Like the rest of the women, I, too, fell in love with the dynamic West Texan — for three days at least.

By no stretch of the imagination could the author-cowman be categorized as a flirt. On the other hand, neither did he discourage overtly the excessive adulation lavished upon him. Undeterred, he went right on adding a new dimension to the concept of Southern chivalry.

Haley had just switched publishers — to Oklahoma University Press — and no doubt they wished to exploit the fact. They exhibited him in the cowman role, attired in expensive and colorful range regalia[3] and demonstrating the border roll spin and the fast draw from the hips, sometimes with one Colt .45, at others with two.

When Haley appeared in regular street clothes, you might have mistaken him for a young financier or an investment broker from Wall Street. Moreover, whether he was giving his favorite recipe for sourdough biscuits, which he had cooked over many a campfire, discussing his books, or extolling the merits of his favorite cowhorses, his voice took on a mesmerizing quality. No wonder Haley was in such demand to make speeches. He had mastered the art.

Born in Belton, Texas, on July 5, 1901, Haley was admirably equipped by background for the role he played as active cowman and range historian. From his parents, the well-known John Haleys, he inherited Southern gentility and a pioneering spirit. His paternal grandfather, Dr. James Haley, a Mississippi planter, migrated to Texas after the Civil War. His maternal grandsire, William (Brazos Bill) Caperton, had been an early Texas herdsman and trail driver. Both grandparents fought for the Confederacy in the War Between the States. J. Evetts Haley's great-grandfather served with Houston and Rusk at the Battle of San Jacinto. Major David Haley, his great-great-grandfather, saw service in the American Revolution and stood with General Washington at the surrender of Cornwallis at Yorktown on October 19, 1781.[4]

Haley spent his boyhood in Midland, where his family located in 1906, when he was five. The place had a profound effect upon young Haley, and he remembered it later as a "little cowtown . . . satisfied with its bovine status," [5] where local cowboys diverted themselves occasionally by shooting out the street lights. But to the mature man, Midland meant eminently more. It was, he said, "as distinct a section of the great traditional range as ever found its symphonies in jingling spurs; its perfume or favorite fragrance in horsesweat and saddle leather." [6]

The author attended West Texas State College at Canyon and obtained a master of arts degree in history at The University of Texas at Austin in 1926. At the university, he came under the influence of the historian Eugene C. Barker, who later became his close friend and a sort of father figure. Haley acknowledged his indebtedness to the historian in "Where Trails Begin" in his biography of Jeff Milton:

> Whatever merit this book may have is due in large part to my great mentor and generous friend, Dr. E. C. Barker, of the University of Texas, from whom, in one brief classroom course and through long association since, I find that human tolerance and critical historical appraisal can and should go together . . .[7]

Haley paid further tribute to his former professor in his publication *A Bit of Bragging about a Cow*: "This copy inscribed for my old mentor and friend, the finest historian and one of the greatest men I have ever known — Doctor E. C. Barker. . . .''

Following his graduation from the university, Haley was employed for nine years collecting historical documents and other materials for the Panhandle-Plains Historical Society of Canyon and The University of Texas Archives, part of which was subsidized by the Rockefeller Foundation. He earned a solid reputation for his expertise as a research scholar and appraiser of original documents, as well as for his actual writing.

Before the termination of his employment with The University of Texas, Haley was called in for a conference with the president, Dr. H. Y. Benedict. Benedict opened the conference by asking Haley what he intended to do when the Rockefeller Foundation money was exhausted. Even at this early date, Haley realized that some of his political views did not coincide with those of the powers that be. Expecting to be fired, Haley had already sent his wife and infant son back to Canyon to await him.

"I've punched cattle for $40 a month," Haley shot back at his august employer without blinking, "and I can do it again!" [8]

It was in 1927 that James D. Hamlin, whose biography, *The Flamboyant Judge,* Haley wrote in 1973, commissioned the author to write the XIT ranch book from records given to the Panhandle-Plains Historical Society by the Capitol Reservation Lands of Chicago. First released under the aegis of the Capitol Reservation Lands in 1929, as indicated, *The XIT Ranch of Texas* was suppressed while a series of libel suits were filed against Haley and the publishers by persons named as outlaws in the text.

Although the defendants won the suits and Haley was exonerated, the book was not reissued for twenty-four years, or until 1953. Haley himself was both proud and relieved at the results of the cases and the fact that some of the earlier adversaries had mellowed during the intervening years.

"It is one of the pioneer works on the early ranches of this section," Haley wrote me on June 21, 1950, while he was working on the new edition, "and seems to have met with the approval of some of the critics as well as the jury that heard the case in the libel suits." [9]

As he explained further in the preface to the 1953 edition, "Back of the Story," by that time many of the principals and cowboys who had participated in the development of the XIT ranch had "loped over the divide[10] . . . to greener pastures." Not only that, Haley felt that the years had "seasoned his judgment." [11]

A later edition, a compressed version, appeared after 1953. But I preferred the edition released by Oklahoma University Press in 1953 — slightly abridged and revised, but uncensored — and my students at Sam Houston State University and I rode the trail with J. Evetts Haley for more than two decades.

We rode that trail where in 1541 Coronado sought the Seven Cities of Cibolo, where Don Juan de Oñate went in quest of the Gran Quivera in 1601, and which the ill-fated Santa Fe expedition crossed in 1841 — the same trail claimed by Spaniards, Mexicans, and Plains Indians long before cowboys and buffalo hunters set boot heel upon it.[12]

It was the trail traveled by both good and bad men: males of heroic mould, like the pioneer cowman Charles Goodnight, who founded the first ranch in the Panhandle; XIT developers Abner Taylor, A. C. Babcock, John V. and Charles Farwell, and the capitol builder, Mattheas Schnell; [13] disreputable characters, like XIT manager B. H. (Barbecue) Campbell and his Maverickers and assorted cattle rustlers and desperados.[14]

It was a lush trail where grama and mesquite grass provided excellent grazing for Plains animals until the resourceful and doughty Texas Longhorns were brought in to be replaced later by thoroughbreds — a deep rutted trace compounded by bog camps, lobos, and prairie fires.[15]

The XIT Ranch of Texas is the saga of barbed wire fencing — 1,500 miles of it that in single strand would have stretched over 6,000 miles. It is the epic of what was once the largest fenced ranching operation in the world — a spread of ten counties in the Texas Panhandle comprising three million acres, which the state of Texas traded for the construction of its capitol. That cavernous but majestic pile of native Texas limestone, erected in 1888 at a cost in materials and labor aggregating $3,744,630.60, still stands in Austin as a memorial to a vanished era.[16]

Haley's first book, dedicated to his cowhorses, remains in a class to itself.

Whereas many books about the West romanticize it — Zane

Grey's, Emerson Hough's, and Will James's, to name a few — J. Evetts Haley's, all meticulously researched and based upon truth, immortalize it.

To Haley, who liked to think of himself as "happily ranging the high trails of history," [17] the subject revolved around people instead of events. From his first biography, *Charles Goodnight: Cowman and Plainsman*, in 1936 (reissued in 1949), to his last, *Robbing Banks Was My Business, The Story of John Harvey*, in 1973, the author demonstrates this philosophy of history.

The list, in addition to Goodnight, Milton, Harvey, and Hamlin, stretching out to include Charles Schreiner, John Armstrong, Bob Beverly, John Baylor, Earl Vandale, George W. Littlefield, Erle Halliburton, Jim East, Quanah Parker, Ranald Mackenzie, and Jim Cook, depicts intrepid men who struggled against extraordinary odds and won. In a very real sense, the books mirror facets of the personality of the author.

Haley considered the Charles Goodnight biography, to which he devoted ten years of research, to be his supreme effort. "The book," said Haley, "is more than the biography of a man — it is the background of my own soil, a part of my tradition." [18] While Al Lowman called the book "a magisterial biography," Savoie Lottinville, who issued the reprint from Oklahoma University Press in 1949, pronounced it "the best Plains biography ever written."

In 1964 Haley published the highly controversial *A Texan Looks at Lyndon*. His son, Evetts Haley, Jr., said it was the only book his dad ever wrote that made him any money.[19] The book became a national bestseller overnight, and four printing houses working concurrently could not supply the demand.

Two and a half months after the first copy appeared, a total of 7,250,000 copies either had been sold or were on order with Haley's printers. Although the publication incited a smear campaign to discredit the author, no conclusions arrived at from the well-documented facts were ever challenged.[20] Chandler A. Robinson has called *A Texan Looks at Lyndon* "one of the most cussed and discussed books of the century." [21]

At a press interview in Los Angeles, California, September 1, 1964, Haley disclaimed that he had written "the study in illegitimate power" (his phrase) as a campaign document. On the contrary, he insisted that he had written it as an academic investigator and historian with an intimate knowledge of the Texas scene.[22]

A few years ago, Haley was invited to spend a day in Austin with the Institute of Texas Studies group sponsored jointly by The University of Texas and the Texas State Historical Association. The director of the event, Joe B. Frantz, expected members of the group, consisting mostly of young teachers, to heckle the author and assumed that Haley would come prepared to defend himself.[23] To Frantz' surprise, Haley spent a delightful day mixing and mingling with the young people who accepted him courteously, even enthusiastically.

When Haley addressed the organization that evening, he held his audience spellbound. In the words of director Frantz, who was also Lyndon Johnson's biographer and champion:

He was beautiful. He was thrilling. He had integrity. He was the highlight of the summer, perhaps even of a lifetime.[24]

This was the J. Evetts Haley who coped with the wind and the sand and the drought along the trail — not an easy rider but a redoubtable one.

This was the Haley who fought to preserve the traditions of the founding fathers, from whom he was descended; to pass on to future generations the legacy of a great republic.

Bookmakers at the Pass:

Carl Hertzog and E. H. Antone

My sparse shelf of books designed by Carl Hertzog does not compare with Alfred Knopf's or Al Lowman's extensive collections. But the books bearing Hertzog's distinctive colophon have special significance for me because two of them are my own. It is also a source of gratification that the books reflect the editorial stamp of Evan Haywood Antone.

Entitled *The Yellow Rose of Texas: The Story of a Song,* the two volumes — a paperback and a hardcover — were published by Texas Western Press, the printing division of the University of Texas at El Paso, in 1971, as monograph number 31 in the institution's nationally acclaimed and prize-winning Southwestern Studies series. The clothbound book, in a limited edition of 300 copies, was the third to be issued since the introduction of the series in 1963.

At the time the books were published, Hertzog was director of the press and Antone, editor. With the progress of the work, the relationship involving publisher, editor, and author became increasingly pleasant as we communicated with each other. One of Hertzog's letters written a month before the books came out reflects his unfailing sense of humor and interest.

52

November 30, 1971

Dear Miss Turner:

Last week I took the complete *Yellow Rose* home and read in bed without interruption. Perhaps I should say I went to bed with the *Yellow Rose* but I am too old for that.

I found the complete package very interesting and easy reading. I think Texana collectors will go for this item. As far as I know nothing much has been done on the *Yellow Rose.*

We are going to get 250 copies bound hardback. Don't know if we can get them before Christmas, but will try.

Sincerely yours,

Carl Hertzog[1]

The softbacks were run off the presses and shipped first. In a letter, under date of December 13, 1971, Antone drew a sketch and provided a description of what the hardcover would look like. The book was to have a yellow linen cover with a die of the rose imprinted in gold and a spine of rose fabric.

When the book appeared, the cover was of the deepest rose-colored linen, with the die of the rose stamped in black and the spine done in yellow. Although the change was attractive, even striking, I wondered why there had been an alteration from the original arrangement. Antone's explanation is interesting:

"Actually, the change was made at the last minute when the bindery discovered it was short of yellow fabric. Mr. Hertzog and I discussed it and decided to go ahead with the colors as used, rather than to delay again to reorder.

"So you see that 'the best laid plans of mice and man [*sic*],' are often changed when faced with reality!" [2]

Hertzog founded the press at El Paso (the Pass). As Antone states in his brochure "Texas Western Press: The First Twenty-Five Years" (1977), "In its beginning, Texas Western Press was both the brainchild and the handiwork of one man: Carl Hertzog, who had joined Texas Western College in 1948 to teach advertising and 'bookology,' a course in book design." [3]

When Hertzog (who was born in Lyons, France, to American parents on February 8, 1902) joined the staff of Texas Western College, his reputation as a creator of beautiful books had preceded him. By the year of his retirement in 1972, he had devoted twenty-four years to the university press and half a century to the profession. In that time, he had designed over 200 books — some for local printers, some free-lance, and others for New York publishers, not to mention countless ephemera such as bookplates, Christmas cards, broadsides, letterheads, and advertising layouts.[4]

Today Carl Hertzog is a legend. Not only is his name synonymous with fine book craftsmanship, his skills in design and typography are recognized throughout the nation.

Many honors have accrued to the famous printer. In 1969 he was inducted into El Paso Historical Society's Hall of Fame. In 1970 his exhibit illustrating the theme "What It Takes to Make a Book" was sponsored by the University of Texas Institute of Texan Cultures at San Antonio. The exhibit toured the Southwest and was admired by thousands.[5] In 1971 Al Lowman compiled a catalogue of the exhibit titled *Printer at the Pass: The Work of Carl Hertzog,* with introductory essays by himself and William P. Holman, another recognized book craftsman. A magnificent specimen of the art, to which the printer himself contributed, the volume is a fitting memorial to Hertzog's genius.

Also in 1970, Betty Smedley, bookseller of Austin, issued her handsome *Carl Hertzog Hope Chest,* Catalogue Number Six, in paperback and in a gold-stamped hardcover, limited edition of 150 copies, in which are listed 166 Hertzog items.[6] The catalogues carry introductory commentaries by Alfred Knopf and Al Lowman.

Hertzog began his career in Pittsburgh with a local job printer. From the outset, he manifested an innate interest in design and began to experiment with it. The painter employs a brush or a knife as his tool of artistry; Carl Hertzog "painted" with the composing stick and employed the principles of geometry and algebra as a means of arriving at proportion of length to width and the determination of page size and symmetry of display.

When the noted printing instructor Porter Garnett saw a broadside that nineteen-year-old Hertzog had designed, he invited him to be his student. For a time, then, Hertzog attended Carnegie Institute of Technology, where he became a protege of Porter.

When Hertzog was twenty-one, in 1923, he accepted employment in El Paso. Advancement came rapidly as he continued to be innovative in his work. The first book produced under his direction was *La Lepra Nacional* by Gonzales de la Parra. It was at this time that the young printer began to contribute articles to *The Inland Printer* and other trade journals, as well as literary publications.

From 1930 to 1944 he had mastered lithography, opened his own small print shop, had met artist Tom Lea and begun to print quality books, and had entered into a partnership with Dale Rester. From 1944 to the dissolution of the partnership in 1947, he produced a number of outstanding books.[7] So, when Hertzog joined the staff of Texas Western College in 1948, he had indeed paid his dues.

Hertzog's long and productive career was punctuated with unusual incidents and situations which he relished recalling. There was the incident involving the first book he released from Texas Western Press in 1952, *The Spanish Heritage of the Southwest*. Because of the Spanish theme of the book, consisting of twelve drawings by artist José Cisneros and text by Francis Fugate, Hertzog decided the cover design should be taken from an adobe brick.

The brick his students brought him for the purpose was too rough to leave an imprint. One of them took the brick home and smoothed it off with a plane. When Hertzog tried inking the planed brick and pulled a proof, sand came up with the ink. Then someone suggested spraying the brick with shellac. The ink came off perfectly.

One day when a visitor accidentally broke a piece off the corner of the brick, which the press director kept on his desk as a memento, Hertzog made an interesting discovery. Not only was the brick composed of bits of straw and chips of rock, it also had in its composition an unmistakable slug of dried horse manure. It was the first time in the history of bookmaking, Hertzog commented, that horse dung was ever used on the cover of a book! [8]

Another incident had to do with *The El Paso Salt War*, published in 1961 for C. L. Sonnichsen, dean of the graduate school. Perfectionist that he was, Hertzog took pains to eliminate the most insignificant typographical error. Ordinarily, his books were relatively free of the so-called "typos."

A sentence in the final paragraph read: "Men can die bravely in a bad cause." After the books were released from the bindery, to Hertzog's dismay, the word *bravely* had somehow been corrupted to *dravely*. Hertzog had the linotypist set up a row of *b's,* and an attempt was made with the aid of scissors and tweezers to correct the error by hand. After the first 100 copies, however, it was abandoned as a hopeless task.

For the next decade, whenever the printer and author, the best of friends, had the slightest disagreement, Sonnichsen would grin and say, "Dravely!" [9]

Still another anecdote dealt with one of Sonnichsen's books entitled *Pass of the North*, the bestseller of 1968 and one of the most popular books Texas Western Press had ever released. The incident in this case occurred before the book was published. A delightful raconteur, Hertzog told the story with characteristic gusto, November 21, 1971, on the occasion of Sonnichsen's installation in El Paso's Hall of Fame. The author had spent thirty-five years researching the text, and Hertzog considered it one of his masterpieces in design and typography.

Sonnichsen had just driven up to Hertzog's office in the press quarters to return the day's quota of corrected proof. The director of the press was sitting at his desk when the incident happened. Mrs. Hertzog, who was looking out of a window, was an eyewitness to it.

Sonnichsen parked the car and got out with a roll of galley sheets under one arm and a quantity of page proofs in the other hand. Just as he reached the sidewalk, a strong gust of wind blew his hat off. As he grabbed for his hat, another blast blew the galley strips from under his arm. In reaching for them, he lost his hold on the page proofs. Immediately, he began running after the flying sheets.

Hertzog joined him, retrieving proofs as he ran. Since the proofs were the only copy of the final alterations, the incident could have been a disaster. Fortunately, the two men retrieved most of the galleys but not before some of them had settled in a deep gorge and others had blown across the Rio Grande.

When they finished their work, Hertzog, who had become noted for his one-liners, remarked to Sonnichsen:

"Leland, this book of yours is an instant success. It already has international distribution." [10]

After his retirement in 1972, Hertzog remained on the staff as consultant for a while, which permitted him to work at a more leisurely pace and on his own time. In 1974 he designed the biography of Josephine Clardy Fox, an El Paso art patron who willed the university property valued in excess of $3 million. Ruby Burns wrote the book. The following year, Hertzog designed *The Parramore*

Sketches (1975) by Dock Dilworth Parramore, an Abilene rancher-artist, who was noted for his drawings of Old West scenes. There were a number of other books that bore Hertzog's brand.

A native of Clarksville, Texas, born to Felix and Eva Antone on December 11, 1922, E. H. Antone has been affiliated with the press since 1969.[11] He obtained his Ph.D. in American literature at the University of California at Los Angeles in 1967, where he was granted a teaching fellowship and was closely associated with Leon Howard,[12] the international authority on Herman Melville. Antone joined the English faculty of the University of Texas at El Paso the same year.

Before obtaining his doctorate, Antone pursued a successful career in commercial journalism, from 1947 to 1965, with the Newspaper Printing Corporation consisting of the *El Paso Times* and the *Herald Post*. At the time he resigned he was advertising manager and was in line for further promotion.[13]

A self-made man, Antone worked in the advertising department of the corporation in the daytime and attended night classes at Texas Western College to earn his B.A. and M.A. degrees. The personal and professional association of Hertzog and Antone dated from this time. The Hertzogs introduced Antone to the woman he married, and the families became close.

Antone was handpicked as Hertzog's assistant. The director of the press wanted a Ph.D. in English to work with him, so he talked Antone into accepting the job.

"There is some difference in ordinary Ph.D.s," Hertzog told me, "and one who worked eighteen years for the newspapers, which includes making layouts and writing copy for customers who buy advertising space."[14] Consequently, Antone was not a newcomer to the publishing field, and his four-year internship with Hertzog served him well.

When Antone joined Hertzog in 1969, the institution itself was undergoing transition. As the seventies emerged, Texas Western College had assumed prominence as the University of Texas at El Paso. Joseph Royall Smiley, who had served briefly as president in 1958–59, returned to head the school in 1969. Then in 1972 — the year Hertzog retired — Arleigh Templeton, the former president of

Sam Houston State University, took over the helm at the Pass. Naturally, these events had their impact. When the institution became a university, the press retained its original name to avoid confusion with the University of Texas Press at Austin.[15]

Not only did Hertzog and Antone find it necessary to adjust to these changes, two other important retirements also had their effect. These were those of S. W. Meyers, who had initiated the Southwestern Studies series, and C. L. Sonnichsen, who, like the famous press director himself, had become a campus legend during his forty-one-year tenure.[16]

To mark the latter event, Dale L. Walker wrote a biographical study of Sonnichsen, one of the last publications on which the two bookmakers at the Pass collaborated. Titled *C. L. Sonnichsen: Grassroots Historian,* the book was published as Southwestern Studies monograph number 34. Hertzog is identified in the book as consultant to the press and Antone as editor-director.

As Hertzog's successor, Antone became the moving force behind the press for nine years. In that time, his duties more than doubled, and Texas Western Press evolved into a one-man operation. Antone edited manuscripts, designed the books, supervised them through the press, and handled the marketing.[17] Simultaneously, he retained his professorship in the Department of English, teaching a few classes each semester.

Antone published approximately 100 books, including the Southwestern Studies series, to which he added prestige. Issued quarterly, the publications have a standing list of over 600, including libraries as well as individual subscribers. Southwestern Studies are sold on an average of 7,000 per year to wholesalers, retailers, libraries, and individuals throughout the world. Orders are regularly processed to points in Europe, Africa, and Australia.[18]

Some important titles released under Antone's directorship were *The Ashmunella Rhyssa (Dall) Complex* (1973), by Edward M. Stern; *Three Dimensional Poe* (1973), by Halden Braddy; *John F. Finerty Reports Porfirian Mexico* (1974), by Wilbert H. Timmons; *Pass of the North,* 3rd. edition (1975), by Sonnichsen; *The Catalan Chronicles of Francisco de Moncada* (1975), translated by Frances Hernandez; *Sunward I've Climbed* (1975), by Howard C. Craig; *Higher Education in Mexico* (1976), by Thomas Noel Osborn; *Anti-Slavery in the Southwest,* Southwestern Studies, number 54 (1977), by Lawrence R. Murphy; and *Down Went McGinty* (1977), by Conrey Bryson.[19]

Not only did Antone emphasize the Southwestern Studies, the press, which continued its tradition of publishing Southwestern history under his aegis, began to concentrate on works with wider appeal. For example, in 1977 the press released William Humphrey's *Ah Wilderness! The Frontier in American Literature,* as number 2 in the Literature Series. The expanded range also embraced the discipline of linguistics. An excellent specimen of the genre was *Studies in Language and Linguistics,* which comprised three volumes, the first released in 1969, the second in 1973, and the third in 1977. Another significant title of the category — and a most timely one — was *The Bilingual Education Movement,* coauthored by William F. Mackey and Jacob Ornstein and published in 1978.[20]

One wonders how Antone spread himself thin enough to do the monumental amount of work that he did. In 1969 he wrote *William Farah: Industrialist,* which Hertzog published. While serving in the dual role of director-professor, he taught three graduate courses: Major American Poets, Henry James, and Survey of American Literature to 1860. He also served on the board of directors of El Paso County Historical Society and was president of the organization from August 1979 to December 1980. He was the recipient of a National Endowment for the Humanities fellowship on Modern American Cultural Criticism held in the summer of 1981 on the campus of the University of North Carolina at Chapel Hill.[21]

In September 1981 Antone resigned the directorship of Texas Western Press to return to full-time teaching in the university's English Department.[22]

"I leave TW Press with a feeling of satisfaction rather than of regret. The twelve years have been wonderful and I have produced almost a hundred titles of which I am very proud, including your *Yellow Rose of Texas,* one of our best in our Southwestern Studies," Antone wrote me. "I am at the point in my career, however, when I need to return full time to the English Department and concentrate on certain projects which I want to accomplish." [23]

Bookmakers at the Pass may come and go, but it is doubtful that there will ever be another such team as Hertzog-Antone.

C. L. Sonnichsen and
the Southwest

When C. L. Sonnichsen took a train for Texas in the summer of 1931, with the ink scarcely dry on the paper certifying his Harvard Ph.D. and a Samuel Butler scholarship declined, seventeenth- and eighteenth-century English literature sustained a loss.

The Harvard man had accepted a summer job at the comparatively unknown Texas School of Mines and Metallurgy in El Paso — a far-flung corner of the Southwest — as a temporary position, a stopgap measure, until he could establish himself at an ivy-league university in the East teaching his beloved English literature.[1]

The writing bug had bitten Sonnichsen during his undergraduate years at the University of Minnesota, where he became a close associate of instructor Mary Ellen Chase (later the novelist),[2] and the crawling invertebrate had nipped him again at Harvard. There remained the Samuel Butler study he had envisioned doing with unbridled enthusiasm.[3] Contrary to the old song, the world was not waiting for the sunrise. The world was waiting for C. L. Sonnichsen's study of Samuel Butler's *Hudibras*.

With incredible industry, the graduate *cum laude* from the University of Minnesota had read his way around the room on the top floor of Widener, where the sacrosanct Child Memorial Library at

Harvard was located. Years later he would "still recall the rich, musty, faintly spicy odor of old leather bindings" and how exciting it was to a young man who had just left the sunshine of Harvard Square.[4]

Not without intestinal fortitude, let alone literary pretentions, had he braved the white-bearded lion, formidable English ballad authority George Lyman Kittredge, in his den. Kittredge had asked for a copy of a paper Sonnichsen had written on the absence of ballad elements in the quarrel of ancients and moderns. Before leaving Harvard, Sonnichsen went by the ballad authority's residence and insisted upon having the paper back. The astonished professor surrendered the paper.[5]

Moreover, it was barely possible that Sonnichsen might find something in this Godforsaken outpost in Texas to contribute to his Butler research. But the library of the School of Mines, like the proverbial stepchild, had long been neglected, with its niggardly budget, its two outdated encyclopedias, and sparsity of volumes concerned for the most part with mines and metals. Not only that, Butler material in most American colleges (Sonnichsen was to learn) was exceedingly meager, if not actually nonexistent. Any proper investigation of Butler's *Hudibras* would necessitate residence in England.[6] Nevertheless, this fact did not diminish C. L. Sonnichsen's burning desire to communicate with the world through his pen. The $300 he had won in the Bowdoin Prize competition, before entraining at Boston, had paid for his ticket to El Paso.

The two courses he had been assigned to teach that summer were the English novel and American literature. So he was possibly still consumed with the verities of academic tradition when the first president of the school, John G. Barry, arrived in El Paso to begin his administration with the opening of the fall semester in September.

Sonnichsen had hardly adjusted to El Paso's sand and cactus and sun when President Barry called him in for a conference and informed him that a course in the Life and Literature of the Southwest was being added to the curriculum of the English Department and he was to teach it.[7] A Harvard man and devotee of seventeenth- and eighteenth-century English literature teaching a course involving boots and saddles was unthinkable. In fact, Sonnichsen doubted that there was such a thing as Southwestern literature, and if there were, he knew nothing about it. Nor did he care to learn.

President Barry won the argument, and Sonnichsen began the course. Although he would not realize it at the time, Sonnichsen's assignment to teach the course in Life and Literature of the Southwest typified a milestone — the first in his transformation from the stuffy Harvard scholar into a dedicated Southwesterner and the dean of grassroots historians.[8]

Whereas Professor Sonnichsen had been impeccably efficient — correct, that is — at the outset of his career in El Paso, as the years passed, he evolved into a fascinating human being who became an inspiration to his students. They did not think of him in the formal terms of mentor or professor. He was to them a rare, perceptive person, with just a touch of flamboyance, and they literally flocked to his classes. Whether it was because of the colorful instructor or the exciting contents of the course, or a combination of both, Life and Literature of the Southwest became the most popular course in the history of the University of Texas at El Paso, as the school became in 1967, and Sonnichsen was on his way to becoming a campus legend.[9]

He made of the course an individual experience, indisputably his own. He continually revised and updated the material comprising his syllabi. For instance, he compiled an immense bibliography of Southwestern works — "The Southwest: The Record in Books, [date] Revision," which he reworked periodically and distributed among his students.

He produced his own text for the course. Devin-Adair released it in the summer of 1962 under the title of *The Southwest in Life and Literature: A Pageant in Seven Parts.* The seven parts of the pageant, or the divisions of the anthology, consisted of The Land Itself, Conquistadores, The Spanish Legacy, The Americans Arrive, The Southwestern Indians, Cowboys and Ranchmen, and Bad Men and Peace Officers. Striding through its pages, in addition to the usual interpreters of the Southwest (Erna Ferguson, Alice Marriott, John C. Duval, J. Frank Dobie, Andy Adams, and J. Evetts Haley), are such writers of national stature as Oliver La Farge, Edna Ferber, Marquis James, Paul I. Wellman, Eugene Manlove Rhodes, Conrad Richter, and John W. Thomason.[10] The book's inscription to Sonnichsen's mother reads: "For Mary Hults Sonnichsen, in whom the pioneering spirit is still strong after eighty years."

Like so many professors who write their own textbooks, Sonnichsen felt the need of one to measure up to his own exacting requirements. The anthology received the uniformly favorable recognition in the press that it deserved.

(Of course, the test of any textbook is how well it works as a classroom vehicle. Sonnichsen's book was an excellent text by that measuring stick, particularly for undergraduates. I used it at Sam Houston State University with much success until my course in Literature of the Southwest was elevated to the graduate level and I had my students read books in their entirety instead of excerpts.)

Sonnichsen taught his course informally, without relaxing his high standards, and enlivened it with a humorous and evocative presentation. It was not unusual for him to bring his guitar (on which he performed quite well) to class and accompany himself in the singing of such old favorites as "The Old Chisholm Trail," "Foggy, Foggy Dew," "The Streets of Laredo," "Wabash Cannonball," the multiple versions of "John Henry," or even the semi-modern and interminable "Casey Jones."

If the songs were unexpurgated, he sang them verbatim and encouraged his students to sing along. Frequently, he included cowboy ballads and threw in, now and then, a Mexican *canción* in the original Spanish. To the delight of his students, he sometimes brought to class a sort of neck harness which he had rigged up so as to play the harmonica simultaneously with the guitar.

As the once sacred classics of Child Memorial Library, the historic Boston Common, and the Charles River receded further and further into the innermost recesses of his mind and Sonnichsen became a well-rounded person, he developed a new set of values and a different philosophy focusing on humanity.

He was able to laugh about the tenderfoot he had been when he first arrived. There was the time he discovered a harmless vinegarroon, a ferocious-looking creature clinging to his shower curtain, and shuddered with fear. He recalled with embarrassment that first time he took the Scenic Drive and held a handkerchief to his nose, believing the old myth that the high altitude would cause nosebleed.

As the Southwest environment became an integral part of him, Sonnichsen discovered that there was a great deal to be learned outside of libraries and books, as much as he valued them. He developed a forthright respect for old courthouse records, government archives, deeds, inscriptions on tombstones, census reports, church and family archives, and always the spoken word.[11]

Increasingly, he sought out old-timers who had either witnessed history in the making, participated in it, or were related to persons that had. How exhilarating it was to get out into the streets and meet people, to talk to ancient prospectors, to buttonhole Indians in their native habitat — to feel himself a part of the ebb and flow of the masses.[12]

Natural phenomena — the arroyos, the hills, the rocks — projected new meanings. Contrast in plant and animal life fascinated Sonnichsen — the picturesque and macabre in juxtaposition: the simple, yellow desert flowers and the Spanish dagger sharp enough to impale a person; the shy little desert birds and the coiled rattlesnake, ready to strike. He was mindful of the proximity of the sluggish Rio Grande. Mount Franklin challenged him. The Pass itself became to him a kind of symbol of the international city. Even the sun and sand and cactus, asserting themselves forcefully as elements necessary to the environment, commanded his respect.

Not only did he decide to work with what was available to him in the area insofar as Southwestern history was concerned, Sonnichsen was grateful for the privilege.

An answer to the question of what to write about had been provided by his landlord F. G. Belk, an insurance man formerly of Houston, through simple suggestion. Belk kept regaling his boarder with stories about the early Texas feuds, the Jaybirds and the Woodpeckers clashing in the streets of Richmond and the gunslinging atmosphere of Hempstead, Texas, better known as "Six-Shooter Junction." Sonnichsen became so interested in the subject that he spent a month of his summer vacation in 1933 in Richmond and Houston collecting data on Texas feuds and feuding.[13]

The nearest parallel to feuding in his immediate surroundings was the El Paso Salt War of 1877, and Sonnichsen had begun to investigate it through the channels open to grassroots historians.

Two other events that made the year 1933 memorable were the Harvard man's elevation to the head of the English Department and his marriage to Augusta Jones, by whom he would later father three children: Philip, Mary Augusta, and Nancy.

By 1935 Sonnichsen had experienced his second milestone in his conversion from a Harvard literary snob into a grassroots historian. The stage occurred when he attended a Texas Folklore Society meeting in Austin.[14] No sooner had he appeared on the scene than the organization elected him president. The honor flattered the young professor enormously. Later he learned why he was chosen so peremptorily and without fanfare. For some time the organization had planned to hold a joint meeting at El Paso with the New Mexico Folklore Society; and, as Sonnichsen himself explained it, they "needed somebody on the ground to run the show. The first man from El Paso to show up at a meeting was going to be president whether he liked it or not." [15]

The joint meeting in El Paso later that year was one of Sonnichsen's most cherished memories. Moreover, from that time, folklore has played a vital role in all of Sonnichsen's writings. At the joint meeting of the two folklore societies, Sonnichsen became convinced that folklore and folkways constitute "a branch of history." Furthermore, it pointed up to him that "what people agree to believe about the facts is a fact in itself, often more influential than the reality." [16] It is his belief that the grassroots historian is concerned with folklore half of the time. "Folklore is a form of truth," Sonnichsen states in his Introduction to *Outlaw: Bill Mitchell alias Baldy Russell* (1965), "important to us because it tells us so much more about our unacknowledged selves. By using it, a grassroots historian adds a dimension which his academic brethren can seldom avail themselves of." [17]

Furthermore, Sonnichsen felt that ninety percent of what people do is based on folklore. As he clarifies it, folkways represent folklore in action. "Folklore is what you think about it; folkways are what you do about it." [18]

Sonnichsen reached his third milestone a little later when he replaced J. Frank Dobie, on leave of absence from The University of Texas in the spring of 1936.[19] He had read a few newspaper articles about Judge Roy Bean and his family. But it was not until he came to Austin to teach for Dobie, who fled the capital to escape the pollen that exacerbated his hay fever, that Sonnichsen began to consider Bean a suitable topic for research.

"The reason I picked Roy Bean to research was the fact that he was so easily accessible from Austin," Dr. Sonnichsen wrote me.

"He was in the Southwestern Literature course . . . and Beanville in San Antonio was only a few miles away. So I went to have a look and dug into the files of the San Antonio papers in the newspaper collection at The University of Texas Library and the fat [Bean was plump] was in the fire." [20]

After the Civil War, Bean, who had been in business with a brother in New Mexico, drifted back to Texas and settled in San Antonio, where he married, reared a family, and lived for twenty years. In the area of South Flores Street, still commonly called Beanville, Bean — a jack-of-all-trades — was a freighter, butcher, wood contractor, dairy operator, and saloon keeper. His extraordinary lifestyle, checkered with dubious schemes for making quick money, involvement in lawsuits,[21] and the avoidance of paying his debts, engendered legends and tall tales, many of which were still in circulation when Sonnichsen visited San Antonio in 1936.

Afterward, when Sonnichsen visited Langtry (on the Rio Grande in Val Verde County, where Bean had operated a saloon and held court as the "Law West of the Pecos"), he was even more convinced that the legendary figure was made to order for his treatment and style of writing.[22] By 1939 he had the manuscript ready to submit for publication.

After its rejection by ten of the big Eastern publishers, Sonnichsen submitted the manuscript to Macmillan in February 1942. At the same time Caxton Printers of Caldwell, Idaho — a small but reputable publisher of Western Americana — was preparing *Billy King's Tombstone,* Sonnichsen's first work, for release. A New York agent had kept the latter manuscript for five years before Sonnichsen withdrew it.

Macmillan rejected *Roy Bean* at first, reconsidered it, and published it in the spring of 1943. A phenomenal success, the book went through eight printings, and Devin-Adair reprinted it in 1958.[23]

As Sonnichsen's books were released, Dobie incorporated them into his course. His *Guide to Life and Literature of the Southwest,* revised edition, 1952, lists three: *Roy Bean: Law West of the Pecos* (1943), *Cowboys and Cattle Kings* (1950), and *I'll Die Before I'll Run* (1951). Dobie's annotation: "He [Bean] was more picaresque than picturesque; folk imagination gave him notoriety . . . Three books have been written about him, besides scores of newspaper and magazine articles. The only biography of validity is Sonnichsen's." [24]

Of much greater significance than the reception of the book was that it typified irreversible evidence that the regeneration of a man set in motion twelve years before was complete. Since that day in 1931, when President Barry had called him in for the conference, Southwestern literature, folklore, and history had been Sonnichsen's most absorbing interests. Not only had he forgiven John G. Barry, he was eternally in his debt. [25]

There would be no turning back. After the publication of *Roy Bean: Law West of the Pecos,* Sonnichsen himself declared that his "heart belonged to Texas, New Mexico, and points west, north, and south." [26]

In 1938 Sonnichsen again obliged Dobie by substituting for him on The University of Texas campus, but after that he declined to leave his post at El Paso except in pursuit of his own activities.

By 1948 Sonnichsen accepted a Rockefeller fellowship awarded by the University of Oklahoma to collect materials for a study involving the modern American cattleman. Beginning in Texas, he interviewed cattlemen all the way to Montana on the east side of the Rockies and all the way back on the west side. [27]

Accompanied by his son Philip, he made the trip in a 1941 vintage Packard equipped with provisions, a camp stove, notebooks, and a borrowed tent. The trip covered 15,000 miles and thirteen states and extended over a period of five months. When the two returned to El Paso, Sonnichsen had four loose-leaf binders filled with 700 pages of handwritten notes.

With a tentative title of *The Cattle People,* the book was published under the caption of *Cowboys and Cattle Kings* by Oklahoma University Press in 1950. Although the work went into a second printing within six weeks after it was released, it drew mixed reviews.

Dobie, strangely enough, was among the few who faulted the work. Speaking for the *Saturday Review of Literature,* he took umbrage at Sonnichsen's defense of "the beef-eaters" against Bernard DeVoto. Dobie concluded his stricture with the observation that "the writer with power to reveal ranch people as they are, inside and out, is still to come." [28]

His friend Walter Prescott Webb, on the other hand, acclaimed the book as the publishing event it later proved to be. In an article in the *American Historical Review,* Webb stated:

> He [Sonnichsen] has brought something new in subject matter to the history of the cattle kingdom, and it is unique, without competitor. And it will take a good competitor to surpass his manner and style of execution. . . . Since it is a primary source, there is little for the critic to find fault with. It is appropriate that this authentic book, a distinctive contribution to history and perhaps to literature, comes from the University of Oklahoma Press and with a format creditable to the bookmaker's art anywhere. . . .[29]

Sonnichsen's preoccupation with folklore was so strong that he spent fifteen years investigating the feuding mores of Texans and New Mexicans.

In "The Folklore of Texas Feuds" (*Observations and Reflections on Texas Folklore*), Sonnichsen states: "The traditional customs and beliefs by which a man lives compel him to exact blood for blood. When it came to feuding, the Texas town or family was truly a folk." [30]

Eventually, Sonnichsen's extensive research paid off. After another five years spent in trying to market his first manuscript on the subject, he went on to publish five books involving feud situations. The first, *I'll Die Before I'll Run,* was released by Harper & Brothers in 1951, and the last, *Outlaw: Bill Mitchell alias Baldy Russell,* by Sage Books in 1964.

By 1948 Sonnichsen had amassed an astronomical quantity of material running to 750 pages of typescript and approximately 150,000 words, plus sixty pages of documentation. He had recorded nineteen feuds in detail and mentioned several others. Originally rejected by the University of Oklahoma Press because of length, the stack of manuscript ultimately yielded three books.

In addition to *I'll Die Before I'll Run,* which Harper's insisted upon reducing to nine major Texas feuds, 291 pages of text, and eighteen pages of introduction, Sonnichsen used his prunings in *Ten Texas Feuds* (1957) and in *The El Paso Salt War* (1961).

Ten years after its initial appearance, *I'll Die Before I'll Run* was reissued by Devin-Adair, together with corrections and revisions and illustrations by José Cisneros.

Outlaw was the author's favorite. He had included the Marshall-Truitt affair in Hood County in *Ten Texas Feuds,* but felt that the outlaw Mitchell deserved a book of his own. A fugitive, living under the alias of Baldy Russell in New Mexico, Mitchell was apprehended in 1907 and tried for a murder he had committed thirty-seven years before. Convicted and sent to prison in Huntsville, he escaped in 1914 and lived again on the run until his death in 1928. Mitchell was so tough that he died on his feet in a Douglas, Arizona, hospital.[31]

Sonnichsen attached importance to the book because Mitchell contradicted the stereotype of the bad man of the West. Comstock Books reprinted *Outlaw* in softcover in 1974.

It was inevitable that Sonnichsen would write a book about El Paso. Not only was the town, which Juan de Oñate had named El Paso del Norte — "the pass of the north" — in 1598,[32] Sonnichsen's base of operations, it held special significance for him. For over thirty years he had been gathering material for the book, and his file of notes assumed gigantic proportions.

The manuscript, as he first submitted it to Devin-Adair, ran to 750 pages and over 150,000 words. After an elapse of several months, with no prospect of publication in view, Sonnichsen retrieved the manuscript and gave it to Texas Western Press. Hertzog welcomed it enthusiastically.

Pass of the North: Four Centuries on the Rio Grande was the major publishing event of the press for 1968.[33] Two extraordinary features were the dust jacket, a reproduction of a painting by Russell Waterhouse, and the chapter initials by José Cisneros. These features, combined with Hertzog's expertise in bookcraft, resulted in a specimen of bibliopegic art. Sonnichsen had succeeded in compressing the book to 467 pages. *Pass of the North* won the Texas Institute of Letters award for the year. It went through three editions in a short time, and a fourth was issued in 1981.[34]

During Sonnichsen's forty-one-year tenure at the University of Texas at El Paso, he served as associate professor from 1931 to 1933; as head of the English Department from 1933 to 1960; and as dean of the graduate school from 1960 to 1967. In 1966 he was appointed the Harry Yandell Benedict Professor of English. In 1967, when Sonnichsen reached the mandatory age for administrators to retire, he returned to full-time teaching, including his famous course in Life and Literature of the Southwest.[35]

When Sonnichsen stepped down in 1972, he was presented the Medallion of Merit, the highest award the institution confers and the seventh in its history. The medallion was accompanied by a scroll which read in part:

> Since the summer of 1931 when he came to the Texas College of Mines from Harvard University, his ledger of service as humanistic teacher, administrator, historian, and author is unparalleled in its scope and impact upon the University's history. His natural facility for friendship, unswerving dedication to teaching and scholarship, and his impressive record as author and historian of the Pass, have had the concomitant effect of bringing lasting fame to his adopted Southwest and to the University, as well as to himself. . . .[36]

In addition to the Medallion of Merit, President Smiley awarded Sonnichsen an emeritus professorship of English, along with the first annual Faculty Research Award and the Outstanding Teacher Award of the Standard Oil Company of Indiana Foundation. Sonnichsen had the added honor of delivering the commencement address of May 13, 1972, an essay titled "The Little Blue Flame" that has since been published.[37]

Some people refuse to retire. Such a person is C. L. Sonnichsen. Three days following commencement at the University of Texas at El Paso, on May 16, 1972, he became the editor of the *Journal of Arizona History* and director of the Arizona Historical Society's publications. In addition to editorial and administrative duties, Sonnichsen has been productive in his own right.

While serving as editor of the *Journal,* he has published six books, including *The Ambidextrous Historian* and *Tucson: The Life and Times of An American City.* His *Colonel Green and the Copper Skyrocket,* released in 1974 by the University of Arizona Press, won a Western Heritage Award from the National Cowboy Hall of Fame and Western Heritage Center and a Spur Award from the Western Writers of America.

San Agustin: First Cathedral Church of Arizona, on which he collaborated with George W. Chambers, was released under Arizona Historical Society's imprint in 1978. Texas A&M Press published Sonnichsen's *From Hopalong to Hud: Thoughts on Western Fiction* in the same year and *The Grave of John Wesley Hardin: Three Essays on Grass-*

roots History in 1979. The latter is Number Five in Essays on the American West sponsored by the Elma Dill Russell Spencer Foundation.

Sonnichsen's major scholarly interest for the past decade has been fiction of the West and Southwest since 1918.[38] An avid reader of fiction, he has taught it, written about it, and collected it for several years. He has presented his collection of some 2,000 volumes of fiction to the library of the University of Texas at El Paso.

His latest studies involving Western fiction[39] have resulted in numerous magazine articles covering a wide range of subjects pertaining to the genre and a collection of the best of these in his book *From Hopalong to Hud: Thoughts on Western Fiction.*

He approaches the subject from the position of the social or cultural historian and examines what these novels reveal about the reader and the society in which he lives. This dimension is an added dividend from Sonnichsen's activity as a grassroots historian. He attaches particular significance to the local sources he has become adept at using — newspapers, court records, county records, along with the memories of the countless men and women he has interviewed over the years.

Since 1918, more than 700 serious novels have been published about the four-state core area of the Southwest — Texas, New Mexico, Arizona, and Oklahoma. Taken as a whole, Sonnichsen believes that these books of fiction, together with the commercial Westerns, approximate a regional profile, as well as provide an insight into the national character.

"Even the insignificant and incompetent ones," in his opinion, "reveal more than their authors intend or their readers perceive. They tell us about ourselves — our ideas and prejudices, our unacknowledged desires and fears, the values we take for granted and live by." [40]

Three of the most provocative essays in the book are "Western Fiction: Index to America," "Sex on the Lone Prairee," and the titular selection, "From Hopalong to Hud."

In the first of these, which introduces the book, Sonnichsen explores the Western novel as it mirrors in its metamorphosis the decline of American ideals on a national level. Southern writers speak for the South; Eastern writers, for the East. ". . . But the West belongs to everybody . . . speaks for everybody." [41]

However, the author points out that, along the way, the status of the Western novel has varied. In 1902 Owen Wister's *The Virginian* "divided the high road from the low road of popular Western novels." Writers like Stewart Edward White, Conrad Richter, and Emerson Hough traveled the high road, while Zane Grey, Ernest Boyd, and William McLeod Raine kept the low road congested.

At the end of World War I in 1918, Western fiction experienced another upsurge in both quality and quantity. Such superior writers as Harvey Ferguson, Paul Horgan, and Tom Lea appeared on the scene.

Still, the present-day trend in both reading and writing tastes demands that Western fiction be realistic and tough. Under the pressure many writers have been eliminated. Others have switched, some to popular history. The few survivors have based their success on the treatment of sexual aberration and excessive violence.[42]

In "Sex on the Lone Prairee," which first appeared in *Western American Literature* (May 1978), Sonnichsen comments on the cold, calculating employment of sex as a commercial commodity in Western fiction.

Whereas earlier novelists stopped at the bedroom door, their successors take the reader "through the bedroom into the barn." A flagrant example is Larry McMurtry's *The Last Picture Show*, which was published in 1966 and made into a motion picture. In the novel, zoophily, or bestiality, is a common occurrence in the small town of Thalia, Texas. Sonnichsen believes that McMurtry's purpose is the exploitation of sex for shock value. It is as if he is saying to himself, "This will panic them." [43]

In Marilyn Harris's *In the Midst of Earth* (1969), a character engages in oral sex, then commits suicide. In the Austin writer Shelby Hearon's family chronicle *Now and Another Time*, published seven years later in 1976, a similar scene goes on for hours. All the while author Hearon watches the action with the utmost objectivity.[44]

Chronologically speaking, "From Hopalong to Hud" is but fifty-four years. But it is not the time span that is important. It is the transition that took place within that time span.

For that matter, the cowboy — a major attraction for almost a century — has always been ambivalent. Both writers and readers were themselves ambivalent about him from the start. He had to be part angel and part devil. Perfect heroes are too dull. The only requisite was that he have guts.[45]

So the unheroic cowboy "chaperoned his employer's long-horns up the Chisholm trail and roistered in the saloons and broth-els of Abilene." [46] The stigma remained. Only Andy Adams in *Log of a Cowboy* (1903) endowed the cowboy with qualities of decency.

There's no denying that the urge to pull the cowpuncher off the pedestal was as strong as the impulse was to put him there. This conflict persisted until the 1960s when the nonhero, the anti-hero, and the SOB began to dominate.

Hopalong Cassidy (Clarence E. Mulford's *Bar-20*, 1906) was a hard-drinking, shoot-em-up cowboy — wild, awkward, immature, but occasionally moral. And he was the norm for many years. With six-gun in hand, he became an American legend.[47]

But as the years passed, the changing world affected the West-ern. With the impact of television in the 1950s, the so-called Amer-ican dream died. By the 1960s, the pioneer had been depreciated and his Indian foe glorified. Conventional standards of conduct were discarded. Sexual permissiveness and violence found accept-ance, and the old taboos, retired.[48]

There are many examples of the SOB or antihero in Western fic-tion. As early as 1944 a notable specimen, *Duel in the Sun,* appeared under the signature of Niven Busch. The son of a wealthy and politi-cally powerful father, the central character is not a real cowboy; how-ever, he lacks nothing to be desired as a genuine SOB.[49]

But the masterpiece of SOBs in Western fiction is the antihero Hud of McMurtry's *Horseman, Pass By* (1960), which in the motion picture version took the character's name. Philip French thinks the Texan Hud "represents a perversion of Western ideals, the deca-dent fag end of a tradition." [50] Unfortunately, the publishers be-lieve the novel portrays a realistic picture of ranching as it exists in Texas today.

McMurtry's novel won the Jesse Jones Award of the Texas In-stitute of Letters in 1962. It got the author a Wallace Stegner Fel-lowship at Stanford and a Guggenheim Fellowship, not to mention a teaching job at Rice University. Such a distinguished piece of work would be expected to sell fifty or a hundred thousand copies at least.

According to the taciturn publisher, *Horseman, Pass By* sold "about fifteen hundred copies." [51]

In *The Grave of John Wesley Hardin,* Sonnichsen brings together material first published separately. The third essay, from which the volume takes its title, appeared originally in *Password* 22 (Fall 1977). For seventy years, Texas's most lethal gunman John Wesley Hardin's grave went unmarked. After twenty years of strenuous effort, members of the Hardin Commemorative Association succeeded in placing a marker at the gravesite on September 29, 1965.[52] Sonnichsen's involvement and his ultimate success in bringing the event to fruition spells out an extraordinary story — the final chapter in the John Wesley Hardin legend.

The second essay, "The Pattern of Texas Feuds," is a revision of "The Folklore of Texas Feuds," which appeared in *Observations and Reflections on Texas Folklore,* previously cited. As in the original version, the author devotes attention to the pattern that feuds follow per se and explodes fallacies concerning them left by the novels of John Fox, Jr.

"Blood on the Typewriter" appeared in more formal dress under the title "The Grassroots Historian" in the *Southwestern Historical Quarterly* 73 (January 1979). The essay is a masterful self-portrait, a resumé of Sonnichsen's forty-year career as a grassroots historian. The metaphorical title was influenced by the violence attached to feuding and the author's frustrating struggle for publication.[53] It took seven years to get his first book, *Billy King's Tombstone,* published.

As a grassroots historian, Sonnichsen was motivated by the excitement and risk involved in the "gathering of forbidden fruit" and the satisfaction that he was recording history that would have become lost except for his work.[54]

In investigating the incendiary material, Sonnichsen stood the chance of getting himself shot. Moreover, the experience of several years' duration taught him a great deal about people. There was one feud story that he never published. It was about a feud that reached its climax in 1911 in the village of Coahama, a few miles east of Big Spring, Texas.

In July 1945, as was his custom, he mailed the manuscript for perusal to the person who had provided him with information. The respondent requested that Sonnichsen meet with some members of the family at a designated place "to talk" about the manuscript. Sonnichsen understood and replied that he would omit the story from his forthcoming publication.[55]

The next letter he received said that publication of the story would have "broken the hearts" of some of the descendants of the feuders. The letter dispelled the last vestige of apprehension Sonnichsen might have had about collecting feud material. He knew that if he talked straight and kept his hands in view, he would survive.[56]

Sonnichsen once defined the grassroots historian as "a man who spends his time finding out what nobody wants him to know and he would be better off not knowing." [57] After forty-odd years and several books later, he changed his definition. He thinks of the grassroots historian as "a useful member of the great historical orchestra — a second violin or maybe a piccolo player — inconspicuous but needed to complete the harmony." [58]

Sonnichsen also thinks of himself as a "popular historian" concerned with the adventures of the human spirit. In an article in *The American West,* he points out that academic historians confuse fact with truth.

"Truth is the sum of many facts," Sonnichsen explains, "but in this case the whole is more than a sum of its parts. Truth is the forest and the facts are the trees which keep us from seeing it. . . . To approach reality, a researcher must draw some conclusions, make some deductions." [59]

Sonnichsen is convinced that no man is a historian unless he makes his reader feel.[60]

June 2, 1981, marked the fiftieth anniversary of Sonnichsen's arrival in the Southwest. And as he approached eighty (as of September 20, 1981), he realized more than ever that the fundamental truths of folk history reverberate from the centers of the planet.[61]

Walter Prescott Webb:
Prophet of the Plains

For two copies of *The Great Plains* Dr. Eugene C. Barker, head of the History Department of The University of Texas at Austin, granted Walter Prescott Webb dissertation credit for a Ph.D., which the university awarded in 1932.[1]

Webb, a member of the History Department of the university, had earned his first two academic degrees — his B.A. in 1915 and his M.A. in 1920 — at the institution. Meanwhile, in 1922 he had enrolled for further graduate study at the University of Chicago. A sensitive and introspective man, Webb, who had one of the finest minds of the twentieth century, left without the degree because of extraordinary circumstances.[2]

The Great Plains won the Loubat Prize of Columbia University for the best book over a five-year period and was acclaimed by a national panel of historians, a quarter of a century later, as the most significant work by a living author.[3] Henry Steele Commager pronounced it "the best single-volume contribution in American history between 1900 and 1950." [4]

Later, the University of Chicago was one of the three institutions, including Oxford University of England and Southern Methodist University, to confer honorary degrees upon Webb.

76

Except for visiting professorships, Webb remained at The University of Texas for forty-five years (1918–1963). He was promoted to full professor in 1933 and elevated to distinguished professor in 1952. When Dr. Barker stepped down in 1951, Dr. Webb succeeded him as head of the History Department and bellwether of the general faculty. In 1958 The University of Texas named Webb as one of its four most significant living alumni, along with U.S. Speaker of the House Sam Rayburn, Secretary of the Treasury Robert Anderson, and Mexico's Minister of Italy Ramon Beteta.

Webb's visiting professorships included Stephen F. Austin State College (as the university was then known), University of North Carolina, University of West Virginia, University of Alaska, Rice University, University of Houston, University of London (Harkness Professor, 1938), Harvard University, and Queens College, Oxford (Harmsworth Professor, 1942–43).[5]

Recognized today as his generation's foremost prophet of the frontier and the leading historian of the American West, Webb has been acclaimed throughout the world.

Before his death in 1963, he was working on an experimental project funded by the Ford Foundation — the teaching of history by closed-circuit television, a series on American civilization.

The son of Casner P. and Mary Elizabeth Kyle Webb, Walter Prescott was born on a farm in Panola County, in the deep East Texas piney woods, April 3, 1888. His parents — "destitute products of the Civil War in search of new opportunity" — had migrated from Mississippi to Texas around 1884.[6]

Both parents, avid readers and hard workers, were nonetheless disparate in temperament. A gentle frontier woman, Webb's mother was a Baptist, who read the Bible for spiritual guidance. A severe man upon occasion, Webb's father was an iconoclast who read the scriptures to dispute them.

Casner Webb was a country schoolteacher and itinerant farmer. Self-educated, he "held school" where the big bullies had usually run off his predecessor the year before. Webb recalls an incident in which his father had to defend himself with his bare hands. A male student came at him with a knife, and Casner choked him into submission. The boy's sisters joined the fight, attacking the teacher with a shovel and stick of stove wood. At times

Casner taught these backwoods schools for as little as $10 a month. In the best of times, his salary rarely exceeded $250 a year. Thus it was necessary for him to supplement his income by working at odd jobs for the penurious sum of seventy-five cents or a dollar a day.[7]

Webb's first contact with the frontier began eight years before the frontier closed, when, as a boy of four, he moved with the family to West Texas in 1892.[8] During Walter's childhood, violence persisted, as young men carried knives and guns and feuding was not uncommon.

But it was the western environment that moulded Webb's early temperament and implanted within him the seeds that were to germinate in *The Great Plains*.[9] Not only was he subjected to the environmental extremes peculiar to the area — intense heat in summer, sweeping, devastating winds in winter, long dry spells, flash floods, and the austerity associated with drouth-scarred, arid terrain — he actually witnessed cattle freezing and starving to death. Worse, he observed people, essentially young persons, struggling against raw, unrelenting nature for sheer survival.

When his father homesteaded a quarter section of land (160 acres) in West Texas, in Stephens County, most of the desirable acreage had been taken. Situated in an area known as Cross Timbers, the land was sandy with a red clay bottom and was covered with stumps, scrub oak, and blackjack.

The squalor that attached to the rugged lifestyle even extended to the food the family ate. There was the dish known as "thickened gravy," a cheap substitute for meat consisting of bacon drippings, flour, and water, for which Webb never lost his distaste.

Webb early developed a voracious appetite for reading and found a kind of escape in a vicarious world of books. By the age of five, he had begun to read and demonstrated precocity. His first teacher, Melissa Gatewood Jones, who taught at the one-room school in the community, permitted five-year-old Walter to attend as a courtesy. Apparently, he was too young to enroll officially.

He listened eagerly as Mrs. Jones taught each class, but seemed more interested in geography than anything else. When the teacher could do so without neglecting her regular charges, she permitted little Walter to take part. One day when she asked a young student where he lived, he said, "Texas." When she told him to locate Texas on the wall map, he pointed out South America. Whereupon the five-year-old auditor raised his hand. "He comes a long way to school," said Walter Webb.[10]

But Webb's school attendance was at best sporadic. As the only surviving son in a group of four siblings, he inherited more responsibility than the ordinary farm boy of his day. By the time he was thirteen he was doing the work of a man, frequently laboring in the fields from sunup to sundown. After his thirteenth birthday, he had to withdraw from school for three years to serve as head of the household and run the farm while his father was away during the weekdays teaching school. The fact that his father sustained an accidental injury only added to Walter's difficulties.

The years between the ages of thirteen and seventeen would have been intolerable to Webb without the relief his reading provided. Later he would speak for himself.

> Thus it was that I touched the hem of the garment of the Great Frontier, almost but not quite too late. Because my father was a teacher I had books and became a reader, and as I read I caught a distorted but alluring vision of another world, a world of books, of a room lined with them to the ceiling. At an early age I determined to escape to that other world, to leave the frontier to those more audacious. . . .[11]

Then one day when he was sixteen, an incident occurred that left a lasting impact. By chance he visited the office of the editor of the *Ranger Record* and came into possession of a copy of *The Sunny South*. The entire family enjoyed the sample copy, and Walter prevailed upon his mother to permit him to subscribe to it.[12]

Published in Atlanta, Georgia, and edited by Joel Chandler Harris, the weekly magazine featured such writers as A. Conan Doyle, Gelett Burgess, and Will Irwin and carried segments of Harris's *Uncle Remus*. It also had a letters-to-the-editor column. Webb wrote a brief note to the column editor stating that he was a farm boy ambitious to become a writer but that he had little education and no money. He also mentioned that his father was a crippled teacher.[13] He signed the note with his middle name because his uncle, for whom he was christened, had pretensions to writing. The letter, which appeared in the May 11, 1904, issue, was one that almost any lad seeking a better life might write.

The receipt of first-class mail was rare for the family living in this remote section; besides, a rural mail route had just been established. When his sister brought him a letter, Walter and his father were plowing corn in the recently cleared stumpy field. It was late afternoon and, almost exhausted from hard work under the sweltering sun, he and his father were resting on the beams of their plows. Stamped "Missent," the letter was addressed only to "Prescott, Ranger, Texas, Care of Lame Teacher." The letter might not have reached Webb had the postmaster, a Confederate veteran, not been reading *The Sunny South* before the carrier delivered it or knew Webb's middle name.[14] The letter, written on expensive stationery and bearing a New York postmark, was dated May 16, 1904:

> Dear Junior — I am a reader of the "Sunny South" and noticed your letter in the "Gossip Corner" — I trust you will not get discouraged in your aspirations for higher things, as you know there is no such word as *fail* in the *lexicon of youth* so keep your mind fixed on a lofty purpose and your hopes will be realized, I am sure, though it will take time and work — I will be glad to send you some books or magazines (If you will allow me to) if you will let me know what you like — Yrs truly
>
> Wm. E. Hinds
> 489 Closson Avenue
> Brooklyn — New York[15]

The two began to correspond, and from that time on Webb never lacked for good reading material.

> Then came books on writing and magazines, the best in the land: *The American Boy,* Joe Mitchell Chappell's *National . . .* Lyman Abbott's *The Outlook,* Orsen Swett Marden's *Success,* and others. He encouraged me to write letters of description and narration, and each Christmas came a letter and a tie that was in a class by itself in Stephens County.[16]

Hinds's letters were full of encouragement and glittering details of the New York scene. He had Webb send him occasional essays for criticism.[17] These he would read and return with notes in the margins and suggestions for improvement.

In 1906, pragmatist that he was, Casner Webb made his son a proposition. He had probably observed by this time that Walter would never make a successful farmer. Walter could have a year of study, free of farm duties, in the town of Ranger — provided he would prepare himself to pass the examination for a second-grade

teaching certificate. Casner moved the family to Ranger in antici-
pation of Webb's success.

To Walter Webb it was a contract, and he fulfilled it. Despite
the fact that he was ill and feverish from tonsillitis, he took the examination and passed it. Thus, at the age of eighteen, when many
young men are either graduating from high school or entering college, Walter Webb was teaching his first school for the salary of
forty-five dollars a month.

In time he studied enough on his own to qualify for a first-
grade certificate and advanced to a job that paid seventy-five dollars a month.[18] It was a case of the son following in his father's footsteps. Casner Webb gave up teaching altogether and moved back to
Cross Timbers to devote full time to farming.

Although Walter Webb had vowed to forsake the frontier for a
better world, he became sidetracked. He began to labor under the
illusion that he was experiencing success. Truly, he was wearing
better clothes, earning the respect of his peers, and enjoying a social
life not open to him before. At least he was no longer grubbing up
stumps and plowing corn. Meanwhile, he had continued to correspond with William E. Hinds. Hinds approved Webb's teaching
and asked for details about it.

Finally, on February 9, 1909, when Walter Webb was least expecting it, there came the opportunity to escape the frontier. Hinds
proposed subsidizing a university education for Webb to begin the
following September.[19]

The letter punctured Webb's illusions. "The letter faced me
about," wrote Webb, "and made what I was doing insignificant — a
means only." [20]

Walter Prescott Webb enrolled in The University of Texas in
the fall of 1909. In the absence of sufficient entrance credits and because he was twenty-one, he was admitted on individual approval.
The financial arrangement with his benefactor was that Webb was
to spend his savings first — an amount of $200 — then rely on
Hinds for what he needed. Hinds was not charging interest. Hinds
continued to keep in touch by letter and never failed to send the
check each month. It was understood that Webb would send him
progress reports from time to time.

As provincial as The University of Texas was in 1909, Webb
found difficulty in adjusting to it. His lack of disciplined study in

high school had left him unprepared. Not only that, he found formal classroom routine irksome, and he preferred to do things in his own way and at his own pace.[21]

Although Webb persisted, his grades were mediocre and academic English posed problems. Some of his English teachers considered him substandard in grammar and punctuation. Others considered his themes superficial and contrived. More than once his freshman themes were returned to him marked "unsatisfactory."

Until Webb came under the influence of Lindley Miller Keasbey, a dynamic and controversial history professor in 1910, he went through a year of orientation making poor grades and mostly drifting.[22]

What bothered Webb was that he was not measuring up to Hinds's expectations. That is, Hinds could not possibly be proud of Webb's poor grades. But not once did Hinds lose faith in Walter Webb or admonish him to try to do better.

Webb alternated between university attendance and teaching. At the end of his sophomore year, he withdrew to teach and reduce his debt of $500 to Hinds. Thus, in 1911–12, he was a member of the Bush Knob school in Throckmorton County.

In 1914, when Webb was preparing to enter the university for his senior year, he obtained a temporary job with the state normal school at San Marcos at $150 a month. For an undistinguished undergraduate, the post was flattering. When the man he had replaced suddenly returned after the first quarter, Webb began his senior year at the university, light of heart and with a small bank account. Bolstered by his success, he redoubled his efforts and earned his B.A. degree. But at twenty-seven, with his undergraduate work behind him, Webb was still unable to show Hinds a return on his investment. He was as yet unpublished, even though his grades had improved.

Following graduation, Webb next accepted the post of principal at Cuero High School at $133 a month. As school got under way in the fall of 1915, he received a message that was to affect him for the rest of his life. *William E. Hinds was dead.*[23] Hinds had died without Webb having met him. Webb had suggested visiting him in New York, when he earned extra money as a salesman one summer, but Hinds had advised him to apply the money to his university expenses instead.

Nor did Webb know anything about Hinds except that the man believed in him and was providing money to promote his career. Webb had never been able to understand what Hinds saw in him, but it was obvious that his benefactor believed he had writing ability and was willing to gamble on his judgment.

The fact that Hinds had seen something in Webb was like a magnetic force that held him in check. When he felt like dissipating, was tempted to spend his money foolishly, or considered quitting, the thought of Hinds deterred him. "I could not do it for very long," Webb said, "because there was a mysterious man in New York who trusted me." [24]

And now that mysterious man in New York was dead, while Webb, still smarting under his freshman English teachers' rejection, had written nothing.

Undoubtedly, the shock of Hinds's death was softened by Webb's marriage to Jane Elizabeth Oliphant, September 18, 1916. After marrying, Webb accepted a teaching job at Main High School in San Antonio. One pleasant interlude in an otherwise deteriorating professional situation was the arrival of Miss Hinds, a relative of William, for an extended visit to the Alamo city that fall. Miss Hinds became a frequent guest of the Webbs. From her Webb learned that Hinds had been unmarried, had helped other boys, and had been a more or less indifferent importer of European novelties. Webb was too shy to press for further information.

The teaching position in San Antonio became intolerable. Apparently, there was a personality conflict between Webb and the superintendent. At the end of the first year, Webb accepted a position with the Bees Optical Company as bookkeeper.

Webb was at a crossroad. He became so depressed that he considered leaving the profession to go into business. In this state of mind he scheduled an appointment with a fortune teller, Madame Sckerles.

When Webb appeared for his consultation, half a dozen other clients of the psychic sat waiting in the room. Without knowing Webb's name, Madame Sckerles recognized him and motioned him into another room. She had him sit at a table and state his questions.

Should he quit the teaching profession? The medium looked into her crystal ball. "I see you surrounded by books," she said. "Yes, your life will be with books."

The oil boom was on in Ranger, and Webb wanted to know if oil would be discovered on his father's property. The answer was "No." His father would sell the property, but no oil would be discovered on it.

What sex would his unborn child be? The baby would be a girl. Webb handed Madame Sckerles the fee. She returned half of it. "For the baby," she said.[25]

Before Webb left Main High School, Dr. Frederick Duncalf, history professor of The University of Texas, heard him speak at a meeting of the Texas State Historical Association in San Antonio on the teaching of history in the public schools. Dr. Duncalf was so impressed that he proposed such a course designed to train prospective teachers of history be added to the university curriculum with Webb as the instructor.

Accordingly, on November 11, 1918, Webb returned to the university (where nine years before he had enrolled as a freshman) to teach the course at a salary of $1,500 a year. The job would also permit him to begin his delayed graduate study. Just how much influence the fortune teller's predictions had on Webb's decision to accept the position is conjectural. (All of her forecasting had come true, however. The daughter, whom the family named Mary Alice, had arrived July 30, 1918.)

It is more logical to think that Webb's return to the university was an acknowledgment of an unfulfilled commitment to Hinds, whose death was a constant reminder. It is reasonable, then, to think that Walter Webb returned to the campus with a new sense of direction, despite the temporary suppression of his desire to write by his unimaginative English teachers.

Then one night it happened.

Webb's moment of truth came to him on a dark winter night when torrents of rain beat down on the roof of his stuffy room. It exploded in his brain that night, after his return to the university in 1918, as he sat at his typewriter, pounding out with two fingers an article on the Texas Rangers.

Webb had already learned a great deal about the Texas Rangers: their collaboration with horses in the performance of duty; their pride in their Colt revolvers; their enemies, the Comanches; the kinds of society they represented and defended.

Musing on all of this, it occurred to Webb "that when Stephen F. Austin brought his colonists to Texas, he brought them to the edge of one environment, the Eastern woodland, and to the border of another environment, the Great Plains." [26] The Rangers were pressed into service to defend the settlers against marauding Indians equipped to fight on horseback.

Forest-oriented, the Texans had no weapons suitable for warfare conducted from horseback. As the conflict between the Comanches and the Rangers escalated, Samuel Colt solved the problem. Colt invented the precise weapon adequate for such warfare — the revolver. In the transition that followed, when Americans vacated the woodlands to live on the plains, Texans paved the way, Rangers spearheaded the advance, and the Colt revolver was adapted to the needs of a new life situation.

With the rain drumming in his ears, Webb knew that he had discovered something important — the germ idea for the frontier theme. This concept of Americans deserting the woods to inhabit the plains released Webb from the fetters of academic authority: no longer was he an imitator regurgitating what he read or the stereotyped platitudes from other professors' lectures.

It initiated an independent course of investigation — one that could consume a lifetime as he endeavored to find all the answers to the ever-expanding question:

> What else happened? What other changes took place in the manner of living when thousands of westbound people emerged from a humid, broken woodland to live on the level, semi-arid plains where there was never enough water and practically no wood? [27]

The more he pondered it, the broader it became until it subdivided itself into smaller questions pertaining to many categories relating to the human condition.

> Where timber and grass meet, what change took place in geology? What in botany? In zoology? In anthropology? What in the laws of land and water? What in literature? Having specialized in history, I lacked education, knew neither geology, botany, nor zoology, little anthropology, nothing of law, and not much more of literature. . . . Yet my curiosity about these suspected changes was such that it acted like a fire to burn away the obstacle of complete ignorance. I studied all these subjects in so far as they threw light on the questions. . . . [28]

Thus the Texas Rangers, a frontier institution, led Webb to a region to which Texas belonged: the Great Plains, the last American frontier. So he laid the Ranger theme aside to pursue the broader course.

Webb returned, then, to the frontier that he had wanted to escape in his boyhood. He felt once more the seering winds blow white-hot from the desert. He saw again a trail herd blinded and out of control because of the torture of thirst. Asked by a friend when he began his preparation to write *The Great Plains,* Webb answered that it was at the age of four, when his father "left the humid East [Texas] and sat [*sic*] his family down in West Texas, in the very edge of the open, arid country. . . . There I touched the . . . real frontier; there I tasted alkali." [29]

In his rediscovery of the frontier, Webb found himself. Moreover, The University of Texas, instead of being an avenue of escape, proved to be the door through which Walter Prescott Webb would reclaim his heritage and share it with the world.

Webb earned his master of arts degree without difficulty as he plunged into his frontier research and continued his academic duties. But in 1922 he was thirty-four and not immune from the gentle prodding that he should obtain a Ph.D. He was advised to get the degree outside of the milieu of the home base. Dr. Duncalf inquired about the possibility of a scholarship at Harvard, but that university rejected Webb because of his age. The University of Chicago, less discriminating, accepted him. Reluctantly, Webb took a leave for the study in 1922.

At the end of twelve months, he returned to Texas ill, deep in debt, and without the degree. He had failed to satisfy the doctoral committee administering his preliminary orals. Up to that time he had earned the respect of his contemporaries and was doing well in his course work. Perhaps Webb's biggest mistake was his acceptance of the date of February 20, 1923, for the examination, after only six months in residence.

Undoubtedly, there was cause for censure on both sides. After Webb's return to the Texas campus, the academic grapevine circulated distorted versions of the incident. One account had it that Webb — a man of independent mind but unacademic — simply froze when the committee members began to interrogate him and left the scene of the examination abruptly.[30]

Other versions said that Webb disagreed with the inquisitors and argued with them. Still another claimed that he not only differed with them, he also lost his temper. When the committee thought, for instance, that Southerners colonized Texas for the purpose of creating a slave state, Webb insisted that it was the desire for land that motivated the settlement of the Mexican province. The committee, in turn, accused the doctoral candidate of being a biased Southerner.[31] Whereupon, so the account goes, Webb informed the committee that it was obvious that they did not intend to pass him and that "he really didn't give a damn." [32] Furthermore, the candidate found his interrogators sadly lacking in any knowledge of his field.[33]

It is understandable that Webb found the traumatic experience a depressing topic of discussion. He does refer to it briefly, however, in his essay "History as High Adventure" in *An Honest Preface*. "There should be a moral here," he says, "but the only one I can find is this: Don't take an original idea into a graduate school." [34]

Webb had returned to his post in Austin bent upon pursuing his own intellectual interests at all costs and upon writing history as he viewed it from his native state, not as it appeared in some distant center of learning. He took time to recoup his fortune by collaborating with other historians in the writing of a series of successful textbooks as he resumed his teaching duties and immersed himself in his frontier research.

When *The Great Plains* achieved publication in 1931, Webb, at forty-three, still had not obtained the Ph.D. degree. At this time Dr. Barker suggested that Webb use the book as a dissertation and take the degree at the university. Webb declined. He thought the book was "too big" for that. Besides, he had resolved not to listen to another academic lecture if he could help it.

Barker, however, who fully recognized Webb's magnitude and appreciated his service to the university, was also a resolute, as well as a fair, man. He arranged for the conferring of the degree a year later, in spite of Webb's objections and without Webb's taking additional courses.[35] The whole procedure was executed in good taste, an injustice was righted, and a great man's scholarship recognized.

The Texas Rangers was published in 1935, four years after *The*

Great Plains and eighteen years after it was first started. At some
point Webb reasoned the author must say, "No more research . . .
I will write this damned thing now." [36] The fact that the book was
dedicated to William E. Hinds is relevant.

The manner in which Webb peddled his manuscript sounds
like a tall tale. He showed a portion of it to a Little, Brown editor.
The editor liked it, said he would take it, and offered $500 in ad-
vance. Webb shuffled the sheets back together and started to leave.

"You're going to let us have it, aren't you?" the editor asked.

"Frankly, I'm shopping," Webb told him. "I may let you have
it, but I want to look around first for the best offer."

Next Webb showed the manuscript to Ferris Greenslet at
Houghton Mifflin. Greenslet was enthusiastic. "We'll pay you
$1,000 now, $1,000 on receipt of the completed manuscript, and
another $1,000 on the day of publication. We'll also spend $2,500 in
advertising."

As he left, Webb recalls, "I had to kick a few stars out of my
way, I was riding so high. Houghton Mifflin had invested $5,500 in
me — I knew they'd work hard to get their money out." [37]

A definitive treatment of the subject, the book is a salute to
one of the state's finest traditions — the Texas Rangers — on their
hundredth anniversary. Webb phrases his thesis in this statement:

> . . . The Texas Ranger has been throughout the century a human
> being, and never a mere automaton animating a pair of swagger-
> ing boots, a big hat, and a six-shooter all moving across the prai-
> ries under a cloud of pistol smoke. . . . The real Ranger has been
> a very quiet, deliberate, gentle person who could gaze calmly into
> the eye of a murderer, divine his thoughts, and anticipate his ac-
> tion, a man who could ride straight up to death. [38]

The publication of *The Texas Rangers* also marked Webb's
emergence as a businessman. The fee Paramount Pictures paid him
for the film rights provided him with capital to invest. His first investment was an old church building near the capitol grounds. He
leased the building to the state for several years, then eventually
sold it at a neat profit. [39]

Some of the subsidiary benefits Webb received from the project were the pleasurable excursions he made with members of the
organization. He felt that he could write more effectively after he
had seen a particular site or locale that his writing involved. The

Rangers helped Webb to discover the excitement of the Big Bend country.

The Texas Rangers was reissued in 1965 by University of Texas Press with an introduction by the late President Lyndon B. Johnson. Johnson tells one of Webb's stories that is characteristic. Ranger Captain L. H. McNelly, whose slight build contrasted to that of the typical stalwart Ranger, told his men repeatedly that "courage is a man who keeps on coming on." Johnson adds: "As Dr. Webb would explain to me, 'you can slow a man down like that, but you can't defeat him — the man who keeps on coming on is either going to get there himself or make it possible for a later man to reach the goal.' "

The story applies to Webb himself. The Chicago graduate school slowed him down, but by no means did it defeat him.

Webb's third study, *Divided We Stand: The Crisis of a Frontierless Democracy,* published in 1937, examines the distribution of national wealth in the North, South, and West. Webb had toyed with the idea since the stock market crash of 1929, but he did not begin the actual writing until the Supreme Court ruled against the Agricultural Adjustment Act, thus depriving farmers of the same economic protection granted to industry.

Webb's main thrust was that the North, after the Civil War, gained economic control of the nation and retained it through corporate monopoly. He castigated the North particularly for crippling the South economically. The book influenced Franklin D. Roosevelt to issue the National Emergency Report on Economic Conditions in the South in 1938 and to try to correct the imbalance imposed by Northern corporations upon the section.

Called a Philippic and other derogatory names because of its controversial nature, the book was declared out of print as a means of suppression. After its suppression, Webb restored much of the original manuscript that had been expurgated in the galleys and published the second version himself. The book went into a fourth edition and sold 15,000 copies.

Later, when Webb reexamined the distribution of national wealth, he found that the South and the West had gained and the North had declined.[40]

Meanwhile, as Webb's professional career ascended, his domestic affairs declined. He had hoped that the assignment as Harkness lecturer at the University of London in 1938 would provide an opportunity to revive the waning romance, but the imminence of war in Europe only widened the breech.

By 1942, when Webb accepted the Harmsworth professorship of American history at Oxford, he returned to the continent alone. His only antidote to loneliness and a deteriorating marital relationship was to devote six hours a day to writing. As a public relations aspect of his job, he produced a series of twenty articles on the subject of "England in Wartime" to run in the *Dallas Morning News*. He also wrote fragments of the frontier study, along with an autobiographical sketch in the third person to disguise intimacy.

When Webb returned to The University of Texas in 1943, his domestic problems were compounded by the political situation existing on campus. The Homer Price Rainey controversy and the fight with the regents for academic freedom was fast reaching a climax; and Webb, though not a radical, could not ignore it.

Nevertheless, Webb kept plodding away on *The Great Frontier*. While he wrote fragments of the study at Oxford in 1942–43, he did not make a formal outline for the work until 1950.[41] As early as 1936, when he was writing Chapter 6, "The Crisis of a Frontierless Democracy," which provided the subtitle of *Divided We Stand*, he conceived the central idea for the book. Then in 1938 he organized a seminar around the idea and fourteen years later published the book. It is notable that in his dedication he gives credit to the students of the Frontier seminar he set up at The University of Texas in that year and conducted continually, when he was in residence, until 1952, the year the book was published. It is of further interest to note that he also lists theses and doctoral dissertations of students in his bibliography.

The Great Frontier explores the western hemisphere as a frontier for European expansion and addresses the question: what made the Western World what it is? Or, as Webb phrases it in "History As High Adventure": "What effect did all the new lands discovered by Columbus and his associates around 1500 have on Western Civilization during the following 450 years?" [42]

With the publication of *The Great Frontier*, the concatenation was complete. It was the swelling act of a "mental adventure into an expanding world." Webb had begun with the local aspect in *The Texas Rangers*, he progressed to the regional theme in *The Great*

Plains, from thence he moved on to a national area in *Divided We Stand,* and finally concluded with a thesis of international scope in *The Great Frontier.*

How typical of Webb to say: "Taken together they [the four books] tell the story of the expansion of the mind from a hard-packed West Texas dooryard in the outer limits of the Western World." [43]

In his summation in *The Great Frontier,* Webb states that he had to choose between a definitive study and an introductory one. He chose the latter because

> one lifetime is too short to follow out the ramifications of the concept of the Great Frontier; the task is moreover too much for one mind. I elected to open a subject rather than to attempt to close it.[44]

At the beginning of his Introduction to the fifth printing of *The Great Frontier,* released by University of Texas Press in 1979, the distinguished English historian Arnold J. Toynbee states what Dobie and Bedichek had said many times before: "Walter Prescott Webb was a scholar whose mind went on growing all through his life." The decision of The University of Texas to keep *The Great Frontier* permanently in print is an appropriate memorial to its greatest alumnus and most distinguished professor.

In his career, Webb either edited or wrote more than twenty books and countless articles. Other major works include *The Handbook of Texas* (1952), *More Water for Texas* (1954), and *An Honest Preface and Other Essays* (1959).

Begun in 1939, *The Handbook of Texas,* an immense compilation in two volumes, was sponsored by the Texas State Historical Association and funded by the state legislature and the Rockefeller Foundation. It satisfied the need for a long overdue source for students of Texana.

More Water for Texas is a pragmatic approach to the use of Texas streams as a means of innovative conservation. Well qualified to write on the subject, Webb served as special adviser to Lyndon B. Johnson on water conservation in the South and West, first when Johnson was senator, then later when he became vice-president. The United States Bureau of Reclamation recognized Webb's outstanding service to conservation.

An Honest Preface was edited and published by Joe B. Frantz and other friends of the author to celebrate Webb's installation as president of the American Historical Association (1957–58). One of the most perceptive short biographies of Webb extant is the Introduction by Frantz, Webb's close friend and associate in the History Department.

The text consists of thirteen of Webb's most cogent and facetious essays beginning with the titular selection and concluding with his fine "History as High Adventure."

I enrolled in a history course under Professor Webb at Stephen F. Austin State Teachers College in the summer of 1930. Since the visiting professor did not assign seats, I chose to sit opposite his desk on the front row so as to observe him closely. After we had chosen our seats, Webb made a chart of the seating pattern and checked the roll silently.

Without fuss or ado, he stepped promptly into the classroom at the sound of the bell or a minute before. He walked briskly to his desk, methodically removed his hat, opened his briefcase, took out his books and notes, and began. Sometimes there was a slight cough or a clearing of his throat, but never any small talk or preamble. Customarily, Dr. Webb sat to lecture.

Dr. Webb was not a dynamic instructor. Speaking in measured tones, he lectured from notes, usually with his head down. I cannot remember that he ever smiled. Certainly, he never told a joke or bothered to establish rapport with his students. On the contrary, he was so formal as to appear dyspeptic.

Nor did he rely on attention-getting devices or gadgets. He came to class well prepared, however, and disseminated nuggets of wisdom. Although the course was catalogued as advanced American history, it frequently assumed the proportions of anthropology, or perhaps cosmology would be a more accurate classification, as it related America and Americans to the universe.

The Great Plains would not achieve publication until the following year, 1931. But ideas from it permeated Webb's lectures: the history of the grasses, the Plains as a barrier to the westward movement, Webb's contempt for Spain's exploitation of religion in her struggles to conquer the New World, political radicalism as shaped by adverse conditions of environment.

Webb encouraged respect for ideas. To him facts were insignificant unless they could be translated into meaning. On quizzes he gave essay-type questions and expected answers to conform to the techniques of a beginning, a middle, and an end without being unduly verbose. I do not recall that he ever gave a pop quiz requiring a tricky one-word or stereotyped short answer, as many professors of the time did.

I later learned that Dr. Webb, in spite of his formality in the classroom, was really a generous and sensitive person, who on occasion was capable of exhibiting brilliant flashes of humor.

Webb's interest in aiding indigent students to get an education amounted to a fixation. Throughout his career, he had tried to repay the generosity of William E. Hinds by helping students. There was no way of knowing how many he had helped through school or to establish themselves in business.

A case in point was John Haller, who later became a tree surgeon. Not only did Webb co-sign Haller's note of $150, he gave him and his friends employment at Friday Mountain Ranch until they could find more suitable work and offered Haller a house to live in rent-free.

Later, after Haller enrolled in Webb's seminar course devoted to research on the American frontier, Webb gave him the offer of a lifetime. For his project Haller chose "The Effect of the American Frontier on European Literature." Webb was so impressed with the student's work that he tried to persuade him to expand it into a book. Furthermore, he assured him that he would get it published and offered to subsidize him while he was engaged in writing it. But Webb's young friend had just married and his tree business was beginning to flourish; so he declined the offer.[45]

Webb had an innate sensitivity. There was the time, after Roy Bedichek's funeral in 1959, that he, Glen Evans, and Dobie went to lunch together — a meal none of them really wanted. Dobie's grief was intense. Although Webb had known Bedichek longer than Evans had and was deeply bereft, he took it upon himself to try to comfort the other two friends.

Webb stressed the fact that death had come suddenly and without pain after a long and happy career. While awaiting his wife to announce supper, Bedichek had died of heart failure suddenly in his chair. His fourth book, *The Sense of Smell,* had been accepted and would be published posthumously.

Webb recalled cheerful and witty expressions of Bedichek. He succeeded admirably in raising his friends' spirits. His remarks were particularly comforting to Dobie, Bedichek's best friend.[46]

Another example of Webb's sensitivity involved two children. Asked if he had ever done anything he regretted, Webb admitted that he had. Upon visiting his publishers, Houghton Mifflin, in Boston, he was given a copy of Walter Millis's *The Road to War* to look over. The book's jacket was a vivid red.

Webb went into a park, sat down to rest a moment, and laid the volume on the bench beside him. Two children — a girl of nine and a boy of about five — came up to him. The children were underprivileged and quite dirty.

As the boy neared the bench, he became enchanted with the color of the book and reached his grubby little hand toward it. Dr. Webb pulled the book away. As the incident happened, the little girl admonished the boy. "Don't touch the book," she said. "It's too nice for you."

"I would give anything to live that time over," Dr. Webb explained, "and not to move the book away. It has bothered me for years." [47]

As director of the Texas State Historical Association (1939–1946), Webb initiated the Junior Historian Movement, the publication of books, and the "Texas Collection" section of *Southwestern Historical Quarterly*, the association's official publication. He brought much editorial distinction to the *Quarterly*, but occasionally he was not above interjecting a bit of humor into it.

The "Texas Collection" depended largely upon letters of inquiry and statements of interest from members of the organization for its material. The following request came in the mail:

> Please send me information on the Spanish.
>
> John Doe

Webb ran the request with this reply:

> Please meet the next freight train at the station. We are shipping you the Garcia Library!
>
> Texas State Historical Association[48]

One of Webb's favorite toasts was this given by his fisherman friend of Port Aransas — Florida Roberts. Webb remembered the barefooted Roberts standing on deck, with a can of beer in his hand, reciting the quatrain:

> Here's to the girl that I love best,
> She looks so sweet in her gingham dress,
> But when she's in her pink silk nightie,
> Jesus Christ, God-Almighty![49]

At times, with little prompting, Webb could wax Rabelaisian. One of his favorite stories related to a cowboy who visited a Mexican woman when her husband was out taking care of his cattle.

On one occasion the husband returned unexpectedly during one of the cowboy's visits.

"Queek!" said the señora. "Under the bed. Tony will keel you!"

The cowboy got under the bed just as Tony came through the door.

The ruse was almost successful. A goose sleeping under the bed was awakened by a foot under her wing and suddenly began to hiss.

"To hell with that Aztec!" shouted the cowboy, as he burst from under the bed and ran out of the door in his underwear. "I'm snake bit." [50]

But Webb's keenest demonstration of wit took the shape of satire. Two samples from a talk he made on Dobie at a Texas Folklore Society meeting at the Driskill Hotel in Austin, April 3, 1955, will illustrate.

> His [Dobie's] admiration of Texas sculptors surpasses that for the architects. He thinks the cenotaph on Alamo Plaza in San Antonio is the very embodiment of the artistic spirit of Texas and that the sculptor who made it should be proclaimed an honorary Texas Ranger . . .
>
> Dobie is a total abstainer. He never drinks whiskey except on social occasions, and Dobie is really socially inclined. He does not know the difference between good whiskey and bad whiskey and really shows a strong preference for the most vicious brands. He cannot tolerate Jack Daniels or Old Forrester.[51]

Webb acquired the Old Johnson Institute in the hills southwest of Austin in 1942 and renamed it Friday Mountain Ranch. The property, a 640-acre tract along Bear Creek, was run-down. The grasslands were depleted, the land itself eroded, lacking in humus and devoid of vegetation except for the cedars and a few liveoaks on the hills and broomweeds in the valley.

As Dobie expressed it (in an article for a special edition of the *Texas Observer*), "After Webb acquired the place it entered into his bones — into the very fibers of his being." Immediately he began to invest exorbitant sums of money in its restoration. He spread loads of cotton gin wastage on the grounds to correct the erosion. He used commercial fertilizer on plots of untillable soil. He dammed up Bear Creek, compounding it into a noble pool of water.

But it was the grasses that obsessed Webb. His preoccupation with restoring the grasslands at the ranch amounted almost to monomania. He bought seeds to plant by the bushel. He gathered seeds of sideoats grass, little bluestem, Indian grass, and switch grass and scattered them around the place. He even planned to have title to the land transferred after his death to his friend and business associate, Rodney J. Kidd, to ensure that the turf would be maintained in later years.

In 1960 Webb wrote *Flat Top: A Story of Modern Ranching* and had Carl Hertzog publish it. The book focused on how Charles Pettit converted several thousand acres of impoverished land into a veritable Garden of Eden — an example of model conservation. It could very well have been Webb's own story of Friday Mountain Ranch.

Having succeeded in restoring the water, the soil, and the grass, Webb built barns and animal shelters and stocked his ranch with cattle and swine. He next addressed his attention to the stone house. He considered it an excellent example of early architecture and borrowed $10,000 and restored it as nearly as possible to its original state. Meanwhile, he had requested through his column "Texas Collection" in *Southwestern Historical Quarterly* any information about its original construction.[52]

The house had its own story. Thomas Jefferson Johnson, who founded Johnson Institute in 1852, operated it as a school for girls and boys until 1872. The L-shaped, two-story building consisted of ten spacious rooms, two small ones, and seven fireplaces. Constructed of limestone quarried on the site, and timbers of indigenous cypress and cedars, the house dated from 1853. Girls of the institute had occupied the second floor, while the boys bunked in log cabins with puncheon floors.[53]

Webb's pride in his property was such that in 1942–43, when he was Harmsworth professor of history at Oxford University, he gave his address to the English *Who's Who* as Friday Mountain Ranch, Austin, Texas.

Invariably the champion of humanity, Webb wanted people to benefit from Friday Mountain Ranch. To this end, he directed his business partner Kidd to open a summer camp at the place for boys. From 1949 to 1956, he permitted the Austin public schools to use the property for an annual retreat for boys and girls in a program designed to stress nature study, self-reliance, and respect for the pioneer spirit.[54]

Webb frequently entertained his friends at the ranch. It became the regular meeting place for the campfire suppers which he, Roy Bedichek, and Frank Dobie initiated. For these get-togethers Bedichek brought most of the food, including the steaks and beer, did the cooking, and prorated the cost. These cookouts were strictly stag affairs and nobody was host.

Regulars who attended, in addition to the triumvirate Webb, Bedichek, and Dobie, were Mody Boatright, Wilson Hudson, Hart Stilwell, Frank Wardlaw (after he took over the University Press as director), and John Henry Faulk and Glen Evans, when they were in Austin. Others the regulars brought along were welcome. Governor Coke Stevenson and Homer Price Rainey, president of the university, had been special guests.

Drinking at these affairs was not immoderate. Usually one beer satisfied Bedichek. Webb, who had been abstemious until he was fifty, drank only a glass or two of wine. On other occasions, when inbibing seemed to be in order, he might accept one jigger of liquor, without water. Others conformed in moderation.

If liquor did not flow freely over these campfires, good talk did. As yarnspinners, Dobie and Boatright had no equals. And Webb, now and then, offered competition with a Rabelaisian masterpiece. Glen Evans later recalled:

> The peaceful, open-air setting had an enlivening effect on every member of the supper party. The talk was brisk and witty, and it seemed to improve steadily as the evening wore on. Certainly, the three exceptional men who composed the nucleus of the group and their friends . . . produced the most delightful and enlightening conversation that I have ever heard.[55]

It is possible that a little history evolved from these meetings and ideas for books were gestated. It was around a campfire near

Bear Creek that Rainey first informed his friends that "the regents were out to get him." [56] The colorful champion of human rights Maury Maverick, who added *gobbledygook* to American bureaucratic jargon, was known to have attended.

Perhaps John Henry Faulk, a protege of Dobie's, extracted from his Friday Mountain friends some of his dedication to the philosophy of the liberated mind that evolved in the polemic *Fear on Trial* (1964).

But Friday Mountain's greatest gift to the world of letters was Roy Bedichek's *Adventures with a Texas Naturalist*. Bedichek, who was then sixty-eight, had a book to write. Consequently, in 1946 Webb and Dobie urged him to take a leave of absence from his university duties, seclude himself at Friday Mountain, and write the long overdue book.

To finance the venture Webb, an excellent fund-raiser, and Dobie contacted ten men who donated $500 apiece, the money to be administered by the Texas State Historical Association.[57]

So Bedichek loaded his truck with provisions, paper, typewriter, books and apple crates to hold the books and moved into the stone house at Friday Mountain. A prior intimacy with the environment had its effect.

> The sights, sounds, odors, and, especially, the *feel* of this place stimulate in me memories so warm and intimate that taking up residence here seems more like a homecoming than an escape.[58]

For precisely a year and a day, Bedichek withdrew from urban civilization and, inspired by the natural beauty Webb had helped to create and not averse to the crude accommodations of the stone house, wrote his book. While writing his book, Bedichek did his cooking campfire-style at the open fireplace, and drew the water he used from an outside well equipped with a pulley and bucket. He worked and lived in one room — and with nature.

The big round table, which he set before the fireplace to serve all of his needs, was one that Captain Ernest Best of the Texas Rangers took out of a gambling dive.

> Mine is a second-story room, twenty-two by twenty-three feet, with four windows [Bedichek wrote], each as wide as a barn door; two south, exposing Bear Creek Valley with Friday Mountain just beyond, and two north, looking up a slope crowned by pioneer stock pens, log cribs, and sheds scattered about among giant

live oaks. . . . I found myself concerned with the looks of my room. I didn't want it spick and span. . . . My ideal was a kind of picturesque disorder.[59]

The "Bedichek Room" is now a part of the spiralling legend.[60]

Friday Mountain Ranch testifies to its own immortality. For over forty years it has demonstrated that history and nature, when brought into accord, may serve well the causes of humanity. Once a great man's private domain, Friday Mountain is today his living monument.

"The Search for William E. Hinds," one of Webb's most compelling essays, was published in *Harper's Magazine,* July 1961, and a condensation of it appeared in *Reader's Digest* the following month. In the article Webb describes the straitened circumstances of his boyhood, how he came to the attention of Hinds, and the problems of his freshman year at The University of Texas. He also appeals to persons who know anything about Hinds to get in touch with him.

John Fischer, Webb's editor, who compressed the article and edited out some of the surcharged emotion, states:

This was really the story of his own beginnings, and of the unknown benefactor who helped Walter to climb up from the cotton patch. In his later years he had become obsessed with the notion that he ought to find out all he could about this obscure and long-dead New York businessman, and to create a literary memorial to Hinds' goodness.[61]

Webb had never been able to understand what motivated Hinds. He himself found it easy enough to write a check for a needy student, whom he could see and know, but, he said,

I still cannot understand how a man in New York City could reach far down in Texas, pluck a tired kid off a . . . stumpy field, and stay with him, without asking questions, for eleven years, until death dissolved the relationship.

He did not live long enough to see . . . that the investment . . . was not a bad one . . . I have been late all my life — and it was not until 1931 that I published my first book. . . .[62]

Why Webb waited forty-five years after Hinds's death to make public acknowledgment of his indebtedness to him is a matter for conjecture. He had mentioned Hinds many times to Dobie and other friends and had dedicated *The Texas Rangers* to him.

It could have been that Jane's death on July 28, 1960, only a year before, had triggered Webb's introspection. A woman with her own special interests, Jane, who had insisted years before upon economic independence (which Webb had provided through the assignment of properties and income), had pursued her separate way.[63] The finality of death precluded any further attempts at marital adjustment. Friends had observed Webb's increasing depression at this time.

At seventy-three, late or not, Webb was a historian of international stature and should have had no regrets. But he himself said, "The greater my success, the greater became my sense of obligation to Hinds." [64]

The long article, accompanied by a photograph of Hinds and a facsimile of that first memorable letter addressed to "Prescott, Ranger, Texas" and a picture of the envelope cancellation, is almost like a report, even though Hinds in the afterworld could not read it.

Webb, who was unorthodox from a religious standpoint and may have placed some credence in the occult (he did visit a psychic in San Antonio and did write a posthumous letter to Bedichek), could have written the essay at this particular time — when there was no doubt about the munificent return on Hinds's investment — from some inner compulsion.

Hundreds of readers responded to the article with letters and checks for the Hinds scholarship fund. After the article was reprinted in the *Reader's Digest,* the volume of mail increased. The establishment of a scholarship to honor the name of Hinds was specified in Webb's will, and his own check for the purpose was found in his wallet when he died. Today on the university campus the fund is administered as the Hinds-Webb Scholarship.

On December 14, 1961, Webb married Terrell Maverick, widow of the late Maury Maverick, congressman and former mayor of San Antonio. The short, happy marriage of Terrell and Walter Webb is one of the tragedies of literary history.

When Maury Maverick died in 1954, part of his legacy to his widow were diaries he had inherited from his aunt and devoted mentor in 1926 — Ellen Maury Slayden. Mrs. Slayden had wanted to subsidize her nephew and namesake's enrollment at Columbia

University to study journalism, but he chose to major in law at The University of Texas instead.[65]

As the wife of Congressman James Luther Slayden, Mrs. Slayden had lived in Washington for twenty-two years. The first society editor of the *San Antonio Express* in 1889 and contributor to New York periodicals and *Century* magazine, Mrs. Slayden was a talented writer and keeper of records. A remarkable woman and the social arbiter of the nation's capital, she recorded in minute detail the social and political life of Washington, D.C., from 1897 to 1919.[66]

Mrs. Slayden had converted her notes into a manuscript, with each of the twenty-two years providing a chapter, and expressed to Maverick her desire that it be published. There is evidence that he made some effort to get the work between covers, but on the whole he was too busy to pursue it. In addition to his long career in public life, including tax collector of Bexar County (1930–1934), congressman from the twentieth district (1935–1938), and mayor of San Antonio (1939–1941), he had written two books himself — *A Maverick American* (1938) and *In Blood and Ink: The Life and Documents of American Democracy* (1939) — and countless articles dealing with politics and national affairs.[67]

The late twenties posed other reasons why the time was not propitious for publication of the diaries. Following the stock market crash of 1929, the Depression was imminent, and the second World War was in the offing. Then, too, the revealing nature of the accounts rendered them too indelicate or intimate for exposure during the lifetime of some of the leading national and world figures involved. For all of her reportorial talent and intuitive cognition, Mrs. Slayden lacked objectivity.

For instance, President Theodore Roosevelt's "innumerable relatives" were "so tacky" that it made her like him better . . . Alice Roosevelt had "not quite arrived" and still had "bumptious, awkward manners." [68]

In the Preparedness Parade of 1916, in Washington, "[Woodrow] Wilson never looked more *comme il faut* — white trousers, a short blue sack coat, and straw hat — and he walked with a swagger . . . Were not the eyes of his country and the new Mrs. Wilson upon him?" [69]

Mrs. William McKinley's "poor relaxed hands . . . rested on

her lap as if too weak to lift their weight of diamond rings, and her pretty gray hair cut short as if she had had typhoid fever." [70]

Consequently, the rich material collected dust as a part of Maverick's immense collection of books, manuscripts, letters, and papers until Terrell Maverick called the attention of her friend, the distinguished historian, Dr. Webb, to it in 1961.

In 1958, when Richard B. Henderson was examining the collection for a political biography of Maverick, he discovered the "small pencil-written notebooks" in the mass of material and "proclaimed them 'a historian's dream.' " [71]

Before her marriage to Webb in 1961, Terrell Maverick transferred the Maverick collection to The University of Texas but withheld the Slayden manuscript for Webb's appraisal. Webb considered it "sensational" and felt that it should be published without delay.[72] Forthwith he began to transcribe the originals and prepare the material for publication. There were names to be identified, references to historical events that required clarification or comment. Subsequently, Webb immersed himself in the project as he continued to follow his academic schedule at the university and fill speaking commitments.

According to his friend Dobie, Webb manifested more interest in the book than in any of his own. "He had never seemed so eagerly active over the publication of one of his own books as he was over publishing *Washington Wife*. . . ." [73]

As Webb's speaking engagements took him through Dallas regularly, his friend Lon Tinkle — book editor for the *Dallas Morning News*, instructor of French literature at Southern Methodist University, and author — usually visited with him during the stopovers at the airport. One night in the summer of 1961, Webb telephoned from Austin that he had an hour's wait the next day and had something special to tell Tinkle.

The special news was that Webb believed he had been successful in persuading Terrell Maverick to marry him that autumn. He was so engrossed in his account of it and so excited that he failed to hear his plane announced. How the two men rushed out of the airport and tried to signal the pilot of the plane to stop, with gangplank removed and propellers whirling, made an exciting story. Braniff's station master solved the problem by putting Webb on another plane.[74] The incident was so amusing that Paul Crume, a former student of Webb's and longtime friend, carried it (embroidered) in his "Big D" column in the *Dallas Morning News*, no doubt to the embarrassment of Terrell Maverick.

And so the two not young but beautiful people were wed, and Webb was ecstatic. He frankly observed to Dobie that his marriage was an "unexpected dividend from life." [75] In the summer of 1962, when he was lecturing at the University of Alaska, and Mrs. Webb had been unable to accompany him (for medical reasons), he sent her an airmail letter every day. Mrs. Webb treasures the letters and may release them for publication.

Friends rejoiced in Webb's newfound happiness. When Glen Evans was in Austin in February 1963, he lunched with the couple at the Night Hawk. Webb talked mostly of the soon-to-be-released *Washington Wife*. It was Evans's first time to meet Terrell and his first time to see the couple together. "His unconcealed devotion to Mrs. Webb," Evans said, "and the joy he derived from her companionship was as pleasing for me to observe as it has been for his many other friends." [76]

In 1962 the publication of *Washington Wife*, on which the couple had collaborated, was indeed a *cause celebre*. Webb's major contribution, aside from technical chores, was an eight-page Introduction, in which he comments on the social and political background of the Slaydens and assesses Mrs. Slayden's work in comparison with similar books of the period.

> *Washington Wife* [Webb states] is among the best contemporaneous records of the period between the Spanish-American War — which announced that the United States was a world power — and World War I, which defined the duties and fixed the cost of holding first place. Ellen Slayden not only recorded the social life of Washington, Texas, and Virginia, but she took note of almost every historical event of importance in the nation.[77]

Webb cites five books that portray the same period, or a portion of it, all worthy of note. They were *The Autobiography of Lincoln Stephens, The Letters of Archibald Butt,* Frederick Lewis Allen's *Only Yesterday,* Mark Sullivan's *Our Times,* and Ike Hoover's *42 Years in the White House.* Not only does Webb rank *Washington Wife* with the quintet, he points out its uniqueness in that it was the only book on the period written by a woman and the only portrayal of national and world affairs giving the feminine point of view.[78]

Terrell Webb's Preface is a concise, informal statement, a personality sketch in which she relates to her first husband and to Webb. She credits Mrs. Slayden with having a major effect on her adult life.

Because of Slayden's congressional race in 1920 and the participation of his nephew Maury Maverick as campaigner, Terrell Dobbs, as she was then, had to move her wedding date to Maury from June to May. The election plunged Terrell Maverick into a new and exciting world:

> . . . it introduced me into a world of politics in which I was to live for many years. From that summer political activities in general and the Democratic primary elections in particular have dominated and enriched my life.
>
> As a congressman's wife I lived the sort of Washington life that Ellen Slayden describes so vividly . . . Like Ellen, I did my share of card leaving, and I stood in line, as she had years before, at White House receptions.[79]

Before the book was published, she realized that the Slaydens were becoming involved in her life once more.

> For a while I thought the Slaydens, now dead for more than thirty years, were going to crop up again in my matrimonial plans, for until Dr. Webb had made the transcripts of the original and placed the story with the publisher I seemed to take a second place. Harper's quick acceptance of the Slayden story put things back in perspective.[80]

At best the statement was made tongue-in-cheek. The favorable reception that *Washington Wife* received was its own reward.

On February 17, 1963, Webb was again in Dallas, where he spoke on the Southern Methodist University campus and visited in the Tinkle home. "I have no more books in me that I want to write," he said. "At my age [he was seventy-four] you live from day to day. Terrell and I aren't waiting to celebrate our anniversaries in terms of years. We celebrate each month. Just last week we celebrated our fifteenth anniversary. I am a happy man, a very happy man." [81]

On the evening of March 6, 1963, J. Frank Dobie and two other friends were guests of Frank Wardlaw. As he greeted his guests, Wardlaw said, "Walter Webb thought he would join us, but he will be late." [82] Following some good talk and "the better adjuncts of water" (Dobie's phrase), the men went to a Mexican restaurant without Webb.

Webb and Terrell had left on the morning of the seventh for a trek to the hill country to promote *Washington Wife*. The first point on their itinerary was Kerrville, where Webb was scheduled to lecture to a library group about the book. On the return trip he would address a retired teachers' meeting in San Antonio and the couple were slated to sign autographs at Rosengren's Book Store that afternoon before driving back to Austin. Webb had appeared on his own university campus about 10:00 A.M. on the seventh to attend to last-minute details and tell his secretary goodbye. Friends observed that he was in an exceedingly jovial mood.

The Webbs had been on a tight schedule, and no doubt were very tired when they left San Antonio. At 6:30 that evening, Webb was killed in a one-car accident, twelve miles south of Austin on Interstate Highway 35. When the vehicle overturned, Terrell, who had been asleep in the front seat, was so severely injured that she required three months of hospitalization.[83]

Ironically, Webb was the victim of the machine — one of his so-called "vernacular arts" mentioned in Chapter 12 of *The Great Frontier*. The irony is intensified by the fact that the project that had enlivened the courtship of Webb and Terrell had contributed indirectly to their tragic separation in the fifteenth month of their marriage.

When the accident occurred, it was actually six days short of the "anniversary" of their wedding date. Fortunately, Terrell and Walter Webb had celebrated their "fifteenth anniversary" early.

That spring the grasses at Friday Mountain were magnificent.[84]

Mody Boatright:
Minstrel and Mentor

He was a fixture on The University of Texas campus at Austin for almost half a century. But you would not have taken him to be a professor, certainly not an English professor and scholar of first magnitude. With his irregular, chiseled features, West Texas stance, and inevitable cigar, he resembled a cattleman, an active drover capable of riding out a sand storm, extricating a bogged steer, or officiating at the birthing of a calf.

To some people, the name Mody Boatright equates with Pecos Bill. To others, Boatright identifies with Gib Morgan. The legendary figures — one a myth of the cattle range and the other an acquired tradition of the oil industry — typify two American folk heroes that made Mody Boatright one of the Southwest's foremost folklorists.

Boatright was born October 18, 1896, in Colorado City, where the cattle industry had deep roots. County seat of Mitchell County and the oldest town between Weatherford and El Paso, Colorado City was the scene of the first white settlement on the site, a Texas Ranger camp in 1877. In 1882, fourteen years before Boatright's birth, when the railheads penetrated the area, Colorado City became the first boom town in West Texas.[1]

Mody grew up in Maryneal, a village twenty miles south of Sweetwater, county seat of Nolan County, where his family located in 1899.[2] A station on the Panhandle and Santa Fe Railroad, Maryneal was the ranching and farming center of the county inhabited by cattlemen who ran their herds on the open range.

Since Boatright's family purchased a ranch in the area and occupied it for eight years before the town plot was filed in 1907,[3] they pioneered the range industry in that part of West Texas. Thus Mody was exposed almost from infancy (he was three when his parents moved to Maryneal) to all facets of range culture. Although Pecos Bill did not break into print until 1923,[4] the mythical cowboy adopted by coyotes on the Pecos River was a vital part of the oral range tradition that was the folklorist's legacy.

Boatright took considerable pleasure in his heritage. "Practically all the tales in this collection came directly from the cattle folk of West Texas, among whom I was raised (not reared);" he wrote later, "and some of them are associated with my earliest memories." [5]

Boatright's parents, the well-known cattleman Eldon Boatright and his wife Frances Ann (McAulay) Boatright, did not limit their interests to the raising of cattle. Both were articulate and well read. His father's tastes in reading ran to history and historical novels. Undoubtedly, he introduced his son early to the novels of Sir Walter Scott. His mother's literary preferences played the scale from Mark Twain to the author of *David Copperfield* and included a fondness for the blind poet Milton. Before Mody was subjected to formal schooling, his mother had acquainted him with some of the classics of both English and American literature.

Since the Boatrights were ranch people living in a remote area, the education of their children was not traditional. Governesses were brought into the home, occasionally the children attended sessions of school in Sweetwater, and at least once four families pooled their funds and constructed a school near the communal corner of their ranches and employed a teacher.[6]

The passing of the open range had a stabilizing effect on West Texas cattlemen, as the lusty ambience of range life mellowed and cotton provided a steady, if less dramatic, economy.

Then, by the time Boatright had spent a year of service in the United States Army in 1917–18, another culture had left its impact on West Texas. Ranger had had its oil boom in 1917, Colorado City would have one in 1920, and others followed as wildcatters and corporations exploited the possibilities for the discovery of oil and revolutionized the economy.

So it was inevitable that Mody Boatright would succumb to the enchantment of the troubadour and oil driller Gib Morgan — both a proponent and exponent of the tall tale — who inspired and disseminated a quantity of folklore comparable to the Crockett legend. Born in Clarion County, Pennsylvania, in 1842, Morgan and his exploits are familiar to Texas, Oklahoma, Kansas, West Virginia, and Pennsylvania — and anywhere oil is produced in the United States or by Americans elsewhere in the world.[7]

Boatright pursued four careers simultaneously: academician, folklorist, author, and editor. After taking a B.A. degree from West Texas State Teachers College in 1922 and teaching at Sul Ross State Teachers College, he became an instructor at The University of Texas in 1926. He obtained M.A. and Ph.D. degrees at the university in 1923 and 1932. He was on the English staff for forty-three years, serving as both professor and chairman of the department from 1952 to 1963. Upon his retirement in 1969, he retained an office on the campus as professor emeritus until his death in 1970.[8]

As a professional folklorist, he was active in both state and national organizations and won numerous honors. As associate editor of the Texas Folklore Society (1936–1943), he teamed with J. Frank Dobie for seven years. As Dobie's successor to the secretary-editorship, from 1943 to 1965, he served twenty-one years, a total tenure of almost three decades.[9] It was Boatright's most productive period. During the time he wrote three books of his own and innumerable articles, in addition to discovering and encouraging new writers.

Boatright probably contributed more to folklore in Texas and the Southwest than any other person. He virtually lived and breathed it. With his doctorate in English literature, he pursued his major interest as a serious student of the humanities. Moreover, he convinced his peers that folklore warranted the same respect as other disciplines of scholarship. He proved also that scholarship need not be dull and lifeless. On the contrary, he — himself an authority on the English novelist Sir Walter Scott, on whom he wrote his doctoral dissertation and published several articles — showed that folklore could be both exciting and challenging.

After the death of his first wife Elizabeth Beck, by whom he had a daughter, he married the artist Elizabeth E. Keefer, in 1931. Betty Boatright, as she came to be known, illustrated her husband's books, and he was exceedingly proud of her talent. The couple were parents of a son.

Thematically, Boatright divided folklore into four areas: the cowboy, the American frontier, the oil industry, and folklore and the folklorist in contemporary society.[10] Both a collector and interpreter, he assumed the role of cultural historian in relation to the genre. But he viewed the four areas as component parts of the social spectrum and never lost contact with the structure as a unified whole.

Of J. Frank Dobie, Boatright said, "He never wished to extract folklore from its social context; he sought, rather, to present it as one important element in a cultural matrix." [11] Boatright might have been speaking of himself.

Boatright gave attention first to the cowboy theme in a collection of tales. He included these in slightly modified form in his first book, *Tall Tales from Texas Cow Camps* (1934), for which Dobie contributed a Preface. "The Genius of Pecos Bill," which Boatright wrote in 1929, provides three Pecos Bill stories that trace his evolution from his genesis to his exodus.

The book gains from Betty Boatright's illustrations, such as Slue-Foot Sue making her debut "ridin' down the Rio Grande on a catfish" and Pecos Bill "a-sittin' on that tornado and a-spurrin' it in the withers." [12]

An authority on the range and an active cattleman had this to say of the book:

> His cowboys talk as cowboys do, and his wit and humor belong to the cow range. The wind and weather, — the everlasting weather, wild animals never classified by zoologists, strange birds, the speed of men and horses, narrow escapes, and the fantastic biography of Pecos Bill . . . are the subjects around which these *Tall Tales* have grown.[13]

In later years, Boatright expanded this phase of his metier to include the development of the cowboy into an American folk hero, whose popular exposure dated from the dime-novel era to present-day television. Two articles specifically relating folk heroes to con-

temporary social thought are "Theodore Roosevelt, Social Dar-
winism, and the Cowboy" and "The American Myth Rides the
Range." [14] The wide scope of Boatright's work entailed a thorough
knowledge of both American and world history.

Since the cowboy related to his environment, the folklorist included the American frontier he inhabited. His inclusion of the
cowboy's habitat demonstrated further Boatright's interest in all
aspects of a larger canvas instead of the separate facets of it. Boatright documents this segment of the study in his fourth book, *Folk
Laughter on the American Frontier,* published by Macmillan in 1949.
Dobie's assessment of the book is worthy of attention:

> Instead of being the usual kind of jokesmith book or concatena-
> tion of tall tales *Folk Laughter on the American Frontier* . . . goes into
> the human and social significance of humor. Of boastings, anec-
> dotal exaggerations, hide-and-hair metaphors, stump and pulpit
> parables, tenderfoot baitings, and the like there is plenty, but
> thought plays upon them and arranges them into patterns of so-
> cial history.[15]

"Frontier Humor Despairing or Buoyant?" supports Boatright's thesis that the frontiersman laughed, not out of despair — as
many thought — to minimize his hardships and to show courage,
but strictly out of "buoyant good humor." Because of the relation
of the tall tale to this phase of folklore, the author includes "The
Art of Tall Lying." Boatright was convinced that the tall tale as the
cowboy and frontiersman nurtured it was a distinctive art form.

Nor was the frontiersman merely a spinner of yarns. In "The
Myth of Frontier Individualism," Boatright holds up to scrutiny
the fallacy that rugged individualism was shaped by the rigors of
the frontier. He explodes the myth for the fabrication that it is and
devotes attention to the total saga into which the frontiersman fit-
ted as an individual.

Folklore of the oil industry occupied Boatright's major attention for several years. His first book on the theme (actually his
third from a chronological standpoint) was *Gib Morgan: Minstrel of
the Oil Fields,* illustrated by his wife and published by the Texas
Folklore Society in 1945.

Recognized as the Munchausen of the oil fields in 1880, Morgan reached his height before his death in 1909.[16] Many of his tales
attest to his supernatural prowess. Cases in point were how he used

a needle and thread for a cable and drill stem to bring in a difficult well, employed his snake Strickie for a drilling cable and his shedded skin for a pipeline, built a hotel with only south and east rooms, and drilled a well on Pike's Peak.

Not all of Morgan's tales involved the oil industry. In western Pennsylvania, where Morgan grew up, game was plentiful and horses considered important. Consequently, it was not surprising that he possessed a long-range rifle that shot salted bullets to preserve the game until he could retrieve it and that his remarkable twenty-two-yard-long mount had "three speeds forward and reverse, which served him well both on the road and on the racetrack." [17]

But Morgan did not confine his extracurricular activities to hunting and racing. He also relished fishing. Take the time when he used a drilling cable for a line, a steamboat anchor for a hook, and a young steer for bait. That Mississippi River catfish he took was so big that the water level fell two feet.[18]

Until Boatright began to research Morgan, the character was comparatively ignored by researchers of native American folk humor. Regardless of its social and economic importance, the oil industry failed to excite the collective imagination of the populace as did lumbering, mining, and cattle raising. As Morgan declined, many of his exploits were falsely ascribed to Paul Bunyan, the mythical lumberjack, who supplanted him.

It remained for Mody Boatright to resurrect Morgan and restore him to his rightful place as hero of the oil field hierarchy. In researching Morgan and reviving his tales, Boatright not only corrected a mistake, he made a contribution to an era.

> Gib Morgan's tales . . . transcend the oil industry. . . . They symbolize the whole era of expanding geographical and industrial frontiers, the era of manifest destiny and spread-eagle oratory, the era in which the folk artists . . . attempted to create a literature commensurate with the events of the time.[19]

Boatright's oil field research culminated in the publication of *Folklore of the Oil Industry* in 1963 and *Tales from the Derrick Floor: A People's History of the Oil Industry* (with William A. Owens) in 1970. It is interesting to note that the former book was published six years before Boatright stepped down from the university English Department and the latter within a year after his retirement.

Both works depended largely on oral sources. Boatright was among the first to exploit the techniques of oral history even before its significance was recognized by professional groups and researchers. Research for *Folklore of the Oil Industry* entailed the interviewing of some 200 people who had participated in oil fields in one capacity or another, in addition to printed material and primary sources.

The tape-recorded recollections are now a part of the rare Oral History of Oil Pioneers in the university archives. (Upon Boatright's death, the family presented the remainder of his oral collection and other materials to the university library.)

Boatright was justly proud of his mastery of the techniques involving oral history. Of his extensive archival collection of tape recordings he remarked characteristically:

"You can't sing it, like the Lomaxes' great collection, but it does have the rhythm of daily life and sometimes a phrase that is inspired." [20]

The folklorist used 1940 for the terminal date of his study as that year marked the end of the old era and the transition the industry underwent as it approached a new generation.

Although Gib Morgan reappears biographically and categorically in *Folklore of the Oil Industry,* he shares honors with two fictitious rivals, Paul Bunyan and Kemp Morgan. A cogent aspect of the text is the segment titled "Popular Stereotypes," including the geologist, the oil promoter, the shooter, the driller, and the landowner.

While both books are in a sense compendia, *Tales from the Derrick Floor: A People's History of the Oil Industry* is — as its title indicates — more orally oriented. Boatright and his collaborator traveled considerable distances to record the stories and experiences as pioneers in the oil industry recalled them. Through the extraordinary accounts of men who worked at Spindletop, McKleskey, and Dad Joiner No. 3, the writers succeeded in recapturing for their readers firsthand the feverish excitement and suspense that marked the tradition.

They heightened the histrionic effect by recreating the spirit of the boom towns with the inrush of such camp followers ("boomers") as the wildcatters, opportunists (so-called "tricksters"), gamblers, and ladies of the evening. Certainly, the seamier side of existence peculiar to the time involving the industry was not neglected.

The authors expanded the material to include the language of the oil patches ("Oil Field Lingo") and something of the tools and machines employed and the men responsible for inventing them.

From still a different viewpoint, *Tales from the Derrick Floor* is a valedictory to the old creative era of tall-tale telling that is past and at least an affirmation of the new, highly mechanized age that replaced it. As it transpired, the book also exemplifies Boatright's final sustained effort and personal farewell because of his untimely death on August 20, 1970. He died from a heart attack that resulted from an automobile accident.

As the frontier closed and the folk faced a new challenge, Mody Boatright adapted himself to the change and began to appraise American civilization in terms of contemporary culture. He discovered that both oral and written tradition borrow from each other in the processes of adaptation and creation. He also found that American people have more social similarities than disparities. For example, Charles Wilson and Walter Reuther, two men of diverse class interests, had at least three things in common as Americans. Wilson thought what was good for General Motors was good for the United States. Reuther was convinced that what was right for labor was right for America. Both men believed in prosperity but believed in gaining it in opposite ways. Both spoke the same language; both believed in the destiny of the nation.

Boatright discovered that tradition is never static even in a preliterate society. Take American blacks, for instance. In subjugation they developed a folklore dependent upon the values accessible to them. Charms supplanted medical services they could not afford. Superstition took the place of the education denied them. They consoled themselves with satirical tales of the white man and with the hope of finally achieving justice when they crossed over the River Jordan.

Later, convinced of the possibility of elevation to the level of the white man's culture, the black man "announces without regret that Uncle Tom is dead — but not Uncle Tom's music, which he will cite with justifiable pride as a major contribution to American culture." [21] This shift in emphasis is evidence of the change folklore undergoes in a literate society.

There are those who will remember Boatright best for his relationship to his colleagues and to students.

No man or woman during the Boatright years at the university commanded more respect for principles of character than he. His associates depended upon him to do the fair and just thing in any emergency. Fearless, he could stand up and be counted when the need arose. He lost the fight for Homer Price Rainey, but he did not hesitate to wage it.

The faith which his coworkers had in him is demonstrated by an incident involving his friend Frank Dobie. At one seemingly interminable English staff meeting, Dobie arrived late as usual. After seating himself in the back of the room, he asked in a loud voice, "Has Mody talked yet?"

"Yes" the answer came back loud and clear. Dobie got to his feet, shook his unruly hair away from his face.

"Well, I second whatever it was that Mody said before I came in and call for the question." [22]

Mody Boatright was a masterful teacher. Informal, he was not averse to telling a joke in class, now and then, or punning when it seemed appropriate. Never did he descend to the risque or stoop to vulgarity, however. In fact, without being in the least comedic, he was a natural born yarnspinner.

Approachable, he sat at the head of the long seminar table at which were seated twelve or fourteen graduate students enrolled in a course catalogued as Studies in American Humor. At the first class meeting, Dr. Boatright had us introduce ourselves. He learned our names quickly. Then he would rotate the seating from time to time so that we could become better acquainted. It appeared that he wanted us to enjoy being in the class.

Instead of calling the roll, he would look around. "Everybody here today?" he would ask. Someone might answer, "Mr. Jones is absent." To which Boatright would reply, "Well, now, I surely hope he's not sick. If he is someone call me, will you?"

Dr. Boatright never lectured from notes — formally, that is. He might extract from an inside pocket an envelope or scrap of paper on which he had made a memorandum.

"Oh, yes, let's see here. I made a note of something I wanted to be sure to include today." It could have been further analysis of "The Big Bear of Arkansas," which he considered a classic, or additional interpretation of Sut Lovingood or Simon Suggs, two of his favorite tall-tale characters in Southwestern humor.

Boatright assumed a conversational tone and talked to the group. He never took the position that anyone should defer to him as professor. Rather, he blended with the group. Frequently, he invited comment. But it was not in the give-and-take relationship of teacher and student. It was more in the manner of person-to-person in a professional relationship. For instance, he might say, "Miss Turner, who teaches Southwestern Lit at Sam Houston, ought to have some notion about that. What do you think about that point, Miss Turner?"

Or he might turn to another student when we were considering the lead story, "Guilty but Drunk," in Franklin J. Meine's *Tall Tales of the Southwest,* and say, "Mr. Decker, you're pre-law, I believe. Could you explain to us the meaning of the legal phrase *nolle prosequi* Judge Brown uses in the final paragraph?"

Of course, Mr. Decker arose magnificently to the occasion and cinched his A.

"Well, always wondered what it meant, but was too darn lazy to look it up," Boatright fabricated. But he got the laugh he wanted.

Dr. Boatright returned papers promptly. Instead of putting grades on them, he would enclose concise critiques, along with questions or comments in the margins.

When he made a semester theme assignment and briefed us on the quality of performance he expected and announced the date the paper was due, he asked for our suggestions. "Is that all right?" or "Is that too much?" Then, "Don't hesitate to come in for assistance. I can usually help you with content or bibliography.

"Now, if that date will push you too much, that can be adjusted. Just let me know." All he wanted, he added, was to have time to meet his own obligation and get his grades in on time.

Mody Boatright was an altruist. Nor did his love of people have anything to do with sentiment or professional necessity. He particularly identified with the student. One of his students said: "He is sincerely interested in other people — what they think, what they are doing, what they hope to do." [23]

Boatright's deep-rooted interest in students affected his official conduct. There was the time before World War II that he was asked to give his position on a report concerning the admission to the university of "students from the fourth quartile." His position favored the student in the light of what the university could help him accomplish instead of judging him by past performance.

> My comments on the reports concerning "students from the fourth quartile" will seem negative. I intend them to be constructive.
>
> In the first place, this is a questionable label to those who understand it and a meaningless one to those who don't. To dub students "bottom-of-their-class" graduates even temporarily does nothing to clarify their problems or spur their achievement. Graduating classes inside and outside Texas differ vastly; to be in the lowest ten percent of some classes may mean as much as being at the top of others. More important, there are all kinds of reasons why a student may graduate at low rank.
>
> The really important problem is defined by other reports and new programs at Texas which emphasize the individual student's experience, objectives, abilities, and personal conceptions of his education. . . . Some of our most distinguished alumni fall in this category of low-rank entrance. . . . There are many faculty members who would be willing to work hard with such people. If I am wrong there, then we should get teachers who are interested. In any case, the SFTFQ report should be buried in the files — or burned.
>
> I do not suggest substituting a come-one, come-all program. I do think that those departments which a freshman student is likely to meet when he reaches the campus should look once at what he did in high school and then get on with the job of helping him do the best he can in college.[24]

But Boatright's profound interest in helping students is best illustrated by an incident that occurred when, at the last minute, he was asked to replace a committee member at a doctoral examination. To prepare himself, he obtained a copy of the student's dissertation only the day before the meeting.

The questioning was average as such procedures go. When Boatright's time to interrogate the candidate came, he handed the student fifty pages of notes. "These," he told him, "may make your work more accurate."

When the meeting adjourned, one member remarked that Mody must have spent most of the night preparing the material for the student.

"Couldn't sleep anyway," Mody Boatright grinned as he left the room.[25]

Bandmaster Charles Lee Hill
and the Good Times Brass Band

Charles Lee Hill never left stateside during World War II, but his music went around the world. Hill pioneered the writing of concert band scores in the jazz-swing context of the Big Band era of the 1940s and 1950s as he elevated native American music from a neo-folk form to sophisticated art. While admitting the influence of Glenn Miller, Duke Ellington, and Count Basie, Hill went on to publish more than fifty original compositions and arrangements of his own in the jazz-swing idiom.

In January 1982, Donn Laurence Mills, representative for the National School Orchestra Association and contributing editor for *The Instrumentalist* magazine, wrote to Hill: "It should give you great satisfaction to know that your music influenced a generation of musicians. What was the attraction? Maybe you just hit the temper of the time. If so, that's a superb accomplishment. Not many composers can boast of such influence." [1]

How did Hill get his start in music? A native of Houston, Hill became interested in music as a boy in Nacogdoches when his family moved there. Walking down a Nacogdoches street one day, he heard a man in an upper story of a building counting time and lecturing on the fundamentals of music. Curious, Hill mounted the stairs and slipped into a chair in the back of the room. With only a smattering knowledge of music acquired from his mother and sister, who played piano, he asked the leader to let him join the newly formed band. The conductor refused at first.

"What instrument do you play, son?"

"Not any."

"Then why do you want to join the band?"

"It seems like fun, and I like band music."

"But, son, we're experienced musicians, and I don't have time —"

"Please, sir," Hill interrupted. "If I can't catch on after two or three meetings, I'll drop out. . . ." [2]

That day Charles Lee Hill climbed the stairs to a new world, a world he created for himself. He chose a clarinet for his instrument because he liked the sound of the horn and his parents could buy one for only thirty-five dollars. In time he bought a tenor saxophone and paid for it by delivering telephone books and doing other odd jobs. Without funds for extensive private tutoring, Hill taught himself after three months of lessons from the town bandmaster. He taught himself by observation, experimentation, even osmosis. He did not hesitate to pick the brains of professional musicians. In later years, he listened to records and radio, attended band and symphony concerts, enrolled in summer band camps and clinics, and studied music scores. Music became an obsession with him — a passion.

By the time he was eighteen, he had not only become the featured tenor saxman and clarinetist in a ten-piece local orchestra headed by Johnny Crawford, he was also providing the band with arrangements. Early in his career he had found an old book on arranging, possibly the only one extant, and had mastered its contents in record time.

The orchestra played for college and country club dances, along with conventions and political rallies. When the fellows were lucky, they were paid as much as five dollars apiece for an engagement. Most often, however, they performed for their evening meal or free tickets to a show they were working. Although Hill's arrangements were better than average, conductor Johnny Crawford — a competent musician himself who doubled on the trombone and banjo — liked to joke good-humoredly about Hill's dedication. For instance, he might introduce Hill whimsically:

"Charley Hill puts a lot of fire in his arrangements, and we put a lot of Charley's arrangements in the fire. . . ."

Or he might introduce a number with tongue in cheek:

"When Charley writes an arrangement, he goes from bar to bar. Here is his staggering arrangement of "Makin' Whoopee." [3]

Hill made a point of meeting name band leaders and arrangers as the bands toured Nacogdoches and surrounding towns. While his fellow musicians were out on the dance floor waltzing or jitter-bugging with their girlfriends, Hill haunted the bandstands, observing and taking notes. Frequently, he brought his manuscript paper along and would ask the conductor or arranger during intermission how to write certain passages for a particular combination of instruments. In this manner, he learned from Count Basie, Harry James, and Duke Ellington. Later, he wrote the first published school band arrangement for Glenn Miller's "In the Mood" and Charlie Barnet's "Cherokee."

As a budding musician, Hill became so proficient on both of his instruments that he was accepted as a charter member of the Stephen F. Austin State University Band before he was graduated from Nacogdoches High School.[4]

As a saxist-clarinetist, Hill worked his way through Stephen F. Austin, from which he took a B.S. degree in 1933. There were no courses offered in band technique at the school then, and Hill insists that most of his knowledge about the teaching of band instruments came from his conductor, J. T. Cox. As an undergraduate, Hill was featured by the university band in extemporaneous solos. He became well known for his work at football games. During the music "breaks," when the band would pause for a few bars, the soloist played improvised arabesques, implying the beat rather than stating it. Hill's versatility was such that at athletic events any time he felt like contributing a hot chorus, he was permitted to "take off."

Hill's first conductor's job was as a replacement for the university director (on leave for postgraduate study) in the summer of 1934. At that time, he was invited to take over the conductorship of the Stephen F. Austin State University Band for a twelve-week public outdoors concert series. By popular demand, he returned to his alma mater the following summer for a similar series of concerts.[5] Since then, he and his bands have returned many times.

Hill increased his learning experience at Overton High School, in the East Texas oil fields, from 1935 to 1942. There he directed two bands — a fifty-five-piece, prize-winning marching unit and a twelve-piece stage band. Both music groups provided him with laboratories to experiment with sounds in applying certain arranging techniques.[6]

More important careerwise, it was at this time that he met and came under the influence of Duke Ellington. Ellington saw one of Hill's unpublished song arrangements and played it on a one-nighter dance tour. Undoubtedly, Ellington's encouragement inspired Hill to seek further professional recognition. Accordingly, in 1939 he completed his first serious jazz-swing composition — a paraphrase of the old cowboy ballad, "Red River Valley," made popular by Red Foley. Since his work was more than an arrangement, he was persuaded to rename it "Red Rhythm Valley."

"Red Rhythm Valley" was featured by the world-famed Hardin-Simmons University Cowboy Band. It was adopted by the Southern Methodist University Mustang Band, which made a rehearsal recording and presented it to Hill. The unpublished manuscript also had the distinction of being rendered at the National Democratic Convention in Chicago in 1940. Despite this encouragement, the composition was rejected by seven major music publishers. "It won't sell . . . won't last . . . it is a fad . . . we are afraid to take a chance on an unknown composer," they chorused.[7]

Military service helped to advance Hill's career. He was inducted into the armed forces of the 90th Division at Camp Barkeley, Abilene, Texas, in March 1942. Before his discharge in October 1945, he had been reassigned to the Eighth Service Command at Fort Sam Houston, San Antonio; to Headquarters Detachment, Eighth Service Command, Dallas, and finally to Camp Fannin, Tyler, Texas.

Hill showed his manuscript to band musicians of a medical unit at Camp Barkeley. One of them, a partner of a small music publisher in California, said the firm was looking for music with a modern sound and suggested that Hill submit it.[8]

After its publication in 1942 by National Educational Music Publishers of Hollywood, "Red Rhythm Valley" became an all-time favorite with military, municipal, and school bands. The music was the first published jazz-swing number to include specific instructions for the interpretation of the various jazz rhythms. For instance, Hill employed the + and ○ symbols to indicate closed and open hand positions at the end of the bell of trumpets and trombones to achieve the do-wah effect. The so-called brass derbies were used by Hill in his swing bands with phenomenal success.

It was also the first musical composition to carry a specimen of an instrumental ad lib improvised chorus (such as Hill had made a specialty of as an undergraduate at Stephen F. Austin), and instructions on the conductor's score as to how to interpret the jazz-swing techniques in the percussion section. The instrumentation shows an indebtedness to Count Basie, particularly in the trombone parts.[9]

In 1946 Volkwein Brothers, Inc., of Pittsburgh, Pennsylvania, bought out the small California publisher and established foreign markets for the jazz-swing composition in Europe and in Great Britain. In 1982 "Red Rhythm Valley" went out of print. But the composition — by this time categorized as a popular standard — is still being performed abroad. Only recently, Hill received an international royalty check and discovered that a band in Bergen, Norway, had added the number to its repertoire.[10]

Hill's multiple time-consuming duties in an army camp, which ran the gamut from base librarian and newspaper work to composing music for a camp musical and conducting the medical detachment orchestra, might have discouraged a less committed and creative person. But the instantaneous success of "Red Rhythm Valley," particularly in United States army camps, became an unbeatable incentive to further goals. On top of all the other chores his public relations assignment demanded of him, Hill edited and distributed a small handwritten newspaper entitled *Three Sheets to the Wind* as a contribution to *esprit de corps*.[11]

But it was during his stint with the headquarters detachment in Dallas that he achieved his peak in his musical career. He succeeded in obtaining a national publisher — Carl Fischer, Inc., of New York — for his second and third compositions, "At the Gremlin Ball" and "Deep in Dixie," both released in 1944, a year before his discharge.[12]

Hill's big break came with the publication of "At the Gremlin

Ball'' in 1944.[13] Publisher Carl Fischer sent a complimentary copy of the composition in a package of music to the United States Army Air Force Band conducted by Capt. George S. Howard. Whether by design or not, Hill's music was at the top of the stack. The title had a special appeal for the Air Force: gremlins were thought to be the diminutive mythical gnomes during World War II responsible for the sabotaging of machinery, especially the dysfunction of aircraft.

From the outset, conductor Howard recognized the distinctive style and originality of the "Gremlin" composition. There was a problem, however. In 1943, when Gen. "Hap" Arnold requested Howard to organize "the best damn band in the world," he personally selected 100 musicians from two opposite categories: former members drafted from the nation's leading symphonies and jazz musicians from name dance bands. Naturally, musicians of the two diverse backgrounds did not always agree on programming and performance. They frequently went to the experts (Gordon Pulis, trombone, from the New York Philharmonic or Joe Morek from the Chicago Symphony) for advice. There was one point, however, on which they were unanimous: the score for the music they played had to be perfect. But the 100-piece band had never included jazz per se in its repertoire before.

Still, the more the musicians considered performing Hill's composition, the more the diverse artists began to respect each other. Suddenly, the music itself became the catalyst that restored their complete unanimity.

They became such converts to the jazz-swing composition that they had a scriptwriter compose a sprightly bit of doggerel as an introduction:

> An aviator while flying high
> Was spellbound by what caught his eye.
> On the wings of his sturdy craft
> Little men both fore and aft
> Were unscrewing bolts and breaking struts
> And generally driving the poor pilot'nuts.
> In apprehension he landed his plane
> And to his amazement found it the same
> As when he first took off in flight.
> So right then and there he started to write
> "The Gremlin Ball," a melodious affair

> About little men who weren't there.
> Now Captain Howard and the Air Force Band
> Not in symphonic splendor grand,
> But a hundred strong in a boogie beat
> Swing "The Gremlin Ball" — well all-reet.[14]

The jazz concert score became an integral part of the band's repertoire.

> It became a fun piece and a time to relax. All kinds of improvisations were introduced by both the symphony musicians and the dance men. It is due to this number that the Air Force Band became known as the most versatile band in the world.[15]

In 1944–45, during its international goodwill tour, the band performed "At the Gremlin Ball" before a combined audience of twenty million people in forty countries on five continents.[16] The score was played at a command performance at Buckingham Palace on July 20, 1950. It was featured in a thirty-minute film, replete with soundtrack, *A Serenade to Britain*, which was translated into sixteen languages and shown in seventeen countries as a goodwill gesture by the United States government.[17] Whenever it was performed, it never failed to receive an enthusiastic reception.

But the greatest reception Hill's "At the Gremlin Ball" had abroad was when the United States Army Air Force Band played a concert in Berlin on June 24, 1951. The concert was held in Berlin's Olympic Stadium before a record-breaking audience of 130,000 Germans.[18] It was the Olympic Stadium Adolph Hitler built in 1936 and from which the American athlete Jesse Owens, winner of four gold meals, emerged an international hero.

Attired in impeccable white dress uniform and black velvet cape, conductor Howard made a dramatic entrance by helicopter. After circling the stadium three times, the pilot put down at the foot of the podium at precisely 8:00 that evening as the final notes of the "Air Force Song" (conducted by Howard's assistant) faded away. Disembarking, Howard removed his cape with a flourish and gave the upbeat to Wagner's "Tannehauser" overture.[19] The ovation that ensued was impressive.

As the concert progressed, each number was warmly received. Near the conclusion, when "At the Gremlin Ball" was performed, the applause was thunderous and sustained. After years of deprivation, the German people, hungry for American music, dropped their inhibitions completely as the composition's theme of liberation became instinctively infectious. They would have danced to the music had it been possible. But the spectators, who had been filing into the stadium since 4:00 that afternoon, filled every inch of standing room, entrance ways, walkways, and even perched on top of the scoreboard. It was no less than fantastic that people who were ostensible enemies in a world conflict should express such unprecedented enthusiasm for American music inspired by that war.

By contrast, when "Auf Wiedersehen" concluded the concert, not a sound was heard. Instead, there was one ignited match, then another, and another, until the immense stadium became a lighted flame in silent tribute. Later, conductor Howard could only describe the Berlin concert as "a night to remember." [20]

The United States Army Air Force Band included the "Gremlin" score in its official album for World War II, which it distributed free to radio stations and other media over the nation. Other recordings of the music were made, including a Columbia Records version for a Japanese audience in the 1950s, with Col. Samuel Kurtz, another Air Force officer, conducting. Both television and radio networks performed the number.

Today, "At the Gremlin Ball" is an acknowledged American classic.

Success had come early for Charles Lee Hill. When he introduced swing to the campus of Sam Houston State University in the fall of 1948, armed with a new master of music education degree from North Texas State — his only formal training in the discipline — he was indeed a young man (only thirty-seven) with not one horn but two. [21]

When Hill organized his jazz courses and took over the conductorship of two bands, the Houstonians and a larger feeder group, he amazed the students. Here was an arranger with a jazz composition on 4-Star Records, a creative artist, as well as instructor, who not only taught music theory from a textbook but demonstrated to students how to play their instruments in the commercial interpretation of popular music.

The Houstonians, an eighteen-piece band which functioned as a lab-swing outfit in addition to being the official university dance band, began making headlines in the state press and attracted the attention of the national music magazine *Down Beat* for its "hot, sweet" sound.[22] Soon the band had almost more bookings than it had time for: school proms, shrine and charity balls, homecomings, hotel dances (the Houstonians played engagements at wildcatter Glenn McCarthy's plush Shamrock Hotel, as the Shamrock Hilton in Houston was then known), and for all kinds of collegiate events.

Hill's reputation as a swing band conductor-composer drew students from out of state. Among the best whom he remembers were Ken Stevenson (trombone) from Sioux Falls, South Dakota; Don Hickman (trumpet) from Chicago; and Zelly Sokoll (piano) from Hall River, Massachusetts. By the same token, he also lost a few to territory and name bands, especially during the summer months when the regulars took vacations. Some of the students returned; some did not. But they all went with Charles Lee Hill's blessing.

As Sam Houston State University's campus jumped, eyebrows in Bible Belt Huntsville were raised at the departure from tradition in music education.[23] There was an interesting development, however. The innocuous Huntsville image of the little old sunbonneted lady, with her knitting and her reticule, ascribed to the somnolent little town by some, disappeared summarily.

What some of the longhairs did not know was that Hill believed students should first become familiar with the fundamentals of classical music before attempting jazz-swing. He felt that a superior basic knowledge of traditional music contributed vastly to their ability to interpret and improvise.[24] Although essentially self-taught, he had mastered basic music techniques before deciding to become a swing instructor and arranger-composer in the idiom. As a matter of fact, in fulfillment of the requirements for his advanced music degree, he had composed a classical concert score. Titled "Northern Legend," the composition was patterned after a Beethoven symphony.

The years at Sam Houston State were productive.[25] Hill's original compositions — "Prairie Jump" (1946) and "Little Joe the Wrangler" (1947) — were increasingly popular. During his first year on campus, he brought out two additional swing numbers — "Mars at Midnight" and "Little Boy Blues," which became favorites played at football games in the area.

Hill continued to work on arrangements for the Bearkat

Marching Band of Sam Houston as well as his own dance band. In fact, in 1949 he published *Charles Lee Hill's Band Book of Swing Novelties.* The book included instructions for conductor and parts for twenty-nine instruments, along with such original jazz numbers as "Swinging on the Range"; "When the Work's All Done This Fall"; "Conga Din"; "Swing, Miss Genevieve"; "Swinging in the Hall (of the Mountain King)"; "Stop and Go March"; "Time Out for Jazz"; and "Varsity Ramble."

A special feature of the work was the inclusion of ten sports pep-ups. Hill was the first Texas band composer to publish these snappy musical excerpts, of no more than a minute or so playing time, designed to be used during brief time-outs at athletic events. For convenience, these brief tunes were numbered from one to ten and could be repeated as needed. Advertised by the publisher, Southern Music Company of San Antonio, as "The Hottest Band Book for the 1949–50 Sports Season," the book sold for only one dollar for a conductor's copy and forty cents each for individual band parts.[26]

This first collection of pep-up tunes was so successful that the publisher brought out a more complete book a year later. Titled *Sports Time Out Music Folio,* the book included contributions from three collaborators Hill had chosen. Hill's individual numbers included "The Gang's All Here," "Fight, Fight, Fight!" and "We're Gonna Be Happy," among others.

By the time Hill left the university in 1953, he had added two additional compositions — "Dog Daze" and "Hand Me Down My Swinging Cane," together with such popular arrangements as "Twelfth Street Rag"; "All of Me"; "Alabamy Bound"; " 'Way Down Yonder in New Orleans"; "Pennsylvania Polka"; "Side by Side"; "S-H-I-N-E"; "Mississippi Mud"; and Glenn Miller's "In the Mood." [27]

Perhaps Hill's arrangement that best reveals the skills and techniques of transferring the sounds of the big name band to the concert ensemble is one titled "Put on Your Old Gray Bonnet." Recorded by the Houston Municipal Band, it was performed in an outdoor summer concert at Miller Theater in Houston's Hermann Park in the early sixties under the baton of the late Bert Sloan. The arrangement imitates the style of six name bands of recent years and concludes with a redaction of the "Houston Symphony" playing an inspired "Beethoven" arrangement. Unmistakable, in the following order, are the bands of Glenn Miller, Les Brown, Guy Lombardo, Blue Barron, Xavier Cugat, and Lawrence Welk.

Another of Hill's compositions that docur.ents his being "in temper with the times" — to use music editor Mills's phrase — is the impressive "Space City, USA." Published in 1962, the music was dedicated to the Manned Spacecraft Center in Houston, now known as the Johnson Space Center. Like most marches, "Space City, USA," which followed "Swinging on a Satellite" (1960), is written in two keys. It begins in E-flat and ends in the key of A-flat.

The music was rendered by the Lackland Air Force Band to welcome the late President John F. Kennedy, upon his arrival at the Houston Intercontinental Airport, September 12, 1962, to inspect the space center.[28] Hill treasures a copy of "Space City, USA" autographed for him by President Kennedy.

Hill composed the march in 1961 when the Houston Municipal Band played a series of summer concerts in Hermann Park and later taped the music for a television broadcast called "The Land We Love." He took advantage of the opportunity to extend his prestige in the field and also increase his royalties from the American Society of Composers, Authors, and Publishers, of which he had been a member since 1953.

The Houston Municipal Band performed the then unpublished instrumentation under the caption of "The Pride of Houston." When Hill later submitted the score for publication, he changed the title to "Space City, USA" as he felt that the original title was too regional.

Since the music was released by Southern Music Company of San Antonio shortly before President Kennedy was scheduled to arrive, arrangements were made for the band, which was based in the Alamo city, to secure copies direct from the publishers for a quick rehearsal before arriving in Houston. As it transpired, however, because of a breakdown in communications, the band arrived without copies of the score.

When Hill appeared at the airport, inflated with professional pride, to audit the performance of the score for the august occasion, the conductor informed him of the predicament. Luckily, Hill had just received his copies from the publisher and rushed out to his car to procure them. As the band members hastily placed the instrumental parts on their music stands, the conductor handed the baton to Hill! Thus the flabbergasted Hill conducted the Lackland Air Force Band, which read the score from sight, without having seen it previously.[29]

Surprisingly, the musicians caught up the excitement of the occasion, and the performance was impressive. As the music accelerated to a resounding finale, Gov. John Connally's press aide came around and congratulated Hill. "Sousa himself couldn't have done better," he said. Hill breathed a sigh of relief. Air Force One touched down to the final notes of "Space City, USA," and the band members deployed themselves in military formation and switched to "Hail to the Chief" as the president and his entourage entered the air terminal.

On Saturday, September 30, 1978, thirty-four years after *A Serenade to Britain,* featuring Hill's "At the Gremlin Ball," was made, Hill screened it. On that day Col. George S. Howard, USAF (Ret.) and former conductor of the United States Army Air Force Band of Washington, D.C., invited Hill to visit him at the Air Force Village in San Antonio to premiere the thirty-minute film made during the goodwill tour of Europe and the British Isles in 1944–45.

Hill made the trip from Houston in his car. He had heard the Air Force Band perform "At the Gremlin Ball" in New York and on tour in Texas earlier. But this was the first opportunity he had had to see the film and hear the band's performance of the concert composition in this format. Frankly, former conductor Howard was slightly nervous, for he knew that the performance faced its most exacting — and perhaps most knowledgeable — audience. Any fears that Howard had were unfounded.

Hill listened spellbound to the internationally famous pianist Victor Babin's faultless rendition of a Mendelssohn concerto accompanied by the band at a performance in Liverpool's Philharmonic Hall . . . He heard Glenn Darwin, renowned Metropolitan opera star, sing "Il Lacerato Spirato" from Verdi's "Simon Boccanegra" from the Usher Hall in Edinburgh, Scotland . . . Then at the close he audited the magnificent United States Army Air Force Band playing its own arrangement of Charles Lee Hill's concert composition "At the Gremlin Ball" to a packed house in London's Royal Albert Hall. . . .

"Well, what do you think?" asked Colonel Howard.

"It was well worth the four-hour drive from Houston!" said the modest Texas composer who had teamed with Richard Wagner, Felix Mendelssohn, and Giuseppe Verdi to heal the wounds of war.[30]

Today, in his seventies, Charles Lee Hill could rest on his laurels. In addition to his fifty-eight published scores and numerous articles in music journals, he has directed bands in Texas for more than three decades. Besides his two degrees from state universities, he has pursued work toward the doctorate at New York University, along with other courses qualifying him for positions of school administrator and certified librarian.

Hill's work as arranger-composer has been extolled in state and national magazines and in *Who's Who* music publications. His jazz-swing classic "At the Gremlin Ball" has been compared with the best name band instrumentals. Original copies of his compositions and recordings are a permanent part of the special collections of the Steen Library, Stephen F. Austin State University, and the Thompson Room, Sam Houston State. The famed Band of Welsh Guards, which plays concerts over the world, added Hill's "Space City, USA" to its repertoire in 1981 and released a recording of the composition in 1983.

The musician's most recent honor was induction into Stephen F. Austin State University's Band Directors Hall of Fame in 1984, the fourth recipient of the coveted biennial award in the institution's sixty-one-year history.[31] The award carries with it a music scholarship in the inductee's name with the privilege of selecting the student recipient.

It was in 1982, after an absence of some years, that Hill returned to his first love. That year he took up the baton again as conductor of the Good Times Brass Band of Houston. A nonprofit organization, the band was the brainchild of a realtor, Mac Caldwell (baritone) and a naval architect and engineer, Bill Callender (flute and piccolo). Both in their fifties, the two Houston men felt that the old bandstand-in-the-park music was an American tradition worthy of preservation. Accordingly, in the summer of 1981, they took their dust-collecting instruments out of storage and recruited a handful of others like themselves.

The golden age of American municipal bands, roughly span-
ning the era from the mid-nineteenth century to the infant years of
the twentieth, was an integral aspect of small-town musical culture,
and its resurrection is unique. The fact that it was revived in the
city that is the home of the Houston Symphony and Grand Opera,
and one of the most deeply entrenched musical strongholds of the
nation, was in itself a challenge. Fortified only by their dedication
to a vanishing style of music replaced by rock and roll, the beginning group began to collect out-of-print band scores and to meet
from time to time for practice.

Amateurs at the outset, for the most part, they were faced with
one serious problem. They needed a man to front the organization,
a musician preferably experienced and capable of instructing them
in techniques and professional execution.

No one was better qualified than the former bandsman and
composer Hill, then comfortably hidden away as librarian for
Houston's Northwood Middle School. A coincidence brought the
band and Hill together. Caldwell happened to see an article in a
national music magazine that mentioned Hill's composition "At
the Gremlin Ball" and recalled the composer's impact on the generation of musicians following World War II.[32]

Although Hill had maintained contact with the musical world
as a spectator, he had not actively participated in the field since
1966, when he had accepted a position as librarian in the Houston
area school.

Since Hill took over the conductorship of the band, interest
has escalated and membership has increased. The organization
now consists of thirty-five members ranging in age from fifteen to
sixty-seven. It is a sit-down outfit that plays concerts exclusively;
that is, it is not a marching band, nor does it at this time perform
for dances.

Some of the members are from surrounding towns, but most of
them reside in Houston. A heterogeneous group, the membership
actually represents a cross-section of the city and professions so diverse as to include almost everything from an actor to a professional psychic reader.[33]

For a time, as his crowded schedule permitted, Dr. Grady
Hallman, a well-known cardiologist and member of the famous
heart surgical team at St. Luke's Hospital, played baritone and

trombone with the band. Ten years prior to the time, Dr. Hallman had performed with the Houston dance combo composed of doctors and known as "Musical Hearts," in which Dr. Denton Cooley likewise traded in his scalpel temporarily for bass strings.

While a number of the band members have had experience in performing with school, municipal, and military bands, only two earn their living as professionals. They are Rick Crittenden, twenty-five, who directs an orchestra for a private school in Houston, Northwest Academy; and Noah Lee, fifty-four, who conducts a symphony-type orchestra for the Deer Park Junior High School. Crittenden's expertise is drums, all types; when necessary, he can double on trombone. Lee, a Texas transplant, is a dependable saxist and also an instructor of strings. Lee had a career in counselling until his health forced him to step down recently. His major area was working with teenagers. As a practicing psychologist, he maintained a counselling office with a medical clinic in Washington, D.C. for a number of years. Lee has also been active in the educational field, having served as Texas representative for the National Education Association for some time.

French horn player Drew Kloman, sixty, is active in the theater. A native of Pittsburgh, Kloman has lived in Houston ten years. Having begun at the age of five, the veteran performer can hardly remember a time when he was not acting. From school plays he advanced to the role of straight man in burlesque and from there was graduated to leading roles in summer stock and in road companies. His roles of Chester Morris and Farley Granger opened the doors to films and television.

One of his most recent roles was a minor part in the television production "Bill: On His Own," a sequel to the first "Bill" picture for which Mickey Rooney won an Emmy in 1981.

The oldest bandsman of the aggregation, Wilbur Heinsohn, sixty-seven — a retired Houston mail carrier who plays tuba — was in the eighty-five-mile death march of Bataan. As a bass horn player of the Coast Guard Anti-Aircraft Artillery Band of the National Guard, Heinsohn was called to duty in September 1941 and sent to the Philippines. In 1942, after Gen. Douglas MacArthur was covertly transferred to Australia, before the inevitable surrender at Corregidor, Heinsohn was among the prisoners taken. Later he was transferred to Niigata, a port in Northern Honshu on the

Sea of Japan, where he remained incarcerated until the end of World War II.

Though he barely survived the meager rations and other excruciating rigors of his long imprisonment in Japan, Heinsohn is not bitter. One of his consolations at the end of the war was his renewal of acquaintance with Gen. Jonathan Wainright, who had been imprisoned on Formosa and in Manchuria.

Two of the most enthusiastic members of the Good Times Band are the founders, Bill Callender and Mac Caldwell. Callender, the naval architect and engineer, is president. A native of the Texas port city of Beaumont, Callender came naturally by his fascination for ships and shipping. He was also a product of the city's artistic influence, having begun early to perform in its award-winning public school bands. A 1951 graduate of Massachusetts Institute of Technology, Callender has worked with as many as 1,500 designers and draftsmen at one time on various aspects of ship design. He cites the SS *United States* as perhaps the most significant vessel he had a part in building. The naval architect also operates an industrial consulting business.

Baritone player Caldwell, who studied under the former band leader Clint Hackney of Sam Houston State University and erstwhile owner of the H&H Music Store chain, plays several instruments, including drums and banjo. Mac is a member of a banjo ensemble of the Bayou Banjo Club of Houston and is an excellent soloist on that instrument.

His hobby of collecting used musical instruments amounts to an obsession. He cannot resist buying them for bargain prices at flea markets, pawn shops, or from someone's attic. If the instruments are broken or in need of repair, there's no problem. Mac has mastered the skills involved in repairing different types of instruments.

Bill Burkett, Jr., fifteen-year-old student of the Alief school district, is the youngest band member. Trombone players, he and his father, an industrial supervisor, occupy the second and third chairs. The senior Burkett does occasional arranging and has had some experience at conducting. Both father and son are serious musicians, but they do not compete with each other.

The band is not limited to male performers. One of the women, Glenna Fought, thirty, who performs on the flute and piccolo, is a geophysical technician employed in the oil exploration department of Diamond-Shamrock Oil Company as a seismic librarian. Fought grew up in the jazz atmosphere of New Orleans and has played flute since junior high school. She performed on both flute and piccolo in the Louisiana State University band.

Another of the women, Barbara Hoops, fifty-four, shares the third clarinet spot with another musician. Hoops was a free-lance writer in New York until she married and moved to Houston in 1963.

One of the most interesting — a clarinet player — is a psychic, who also does substitute teaching in the Houston schools. For understandable reasons she keeps the two professions in separate compartments.

The musician describes herself as a natural psychic and identifies herself on her business card as a psychic reader. She works with automatic writing and the crystal ball, along with other phenomena of the trade. Moreover, she deals in past, present, and future lives and makes herself available for private readings, as well as parties and company functions. She was the mediumistic channel for "Orthicar" (an extraterrestrial) for inclusion in a book on the coming Piscean age by the author-astrologer Ted George. She has published articles about her work and is the author of the book *Diary of a 'Closet Psychic.'* [34] Also an ordained minister, the woman has demonstrated her expertise for various churches and other organizations in such widely separated cities as Detroit, Michigan; Jacksonville, Florida; and Palm Springs, California.

Recently at rehearsal she stopped by the conductor's stand on her way to her chair. "Quit worrying," she said. "You're going to be all right." That day Hill had gone to his doctor for a routine checkup, but he had not discussed the fact with anyone.

As diverse as they are, when the band members assemble for rehearsal on Thursday evenings in the Guild Room of Saint John the Divine Episcopal Church, ages are forgotten and differences disappear. It is then that a common bond of love for music unites them into a single, dedicated unit.

The organization has performed in downtown Houston and in various sections of the city — Astro Village, Northwest Mall, Sharpstown — as well as in parks. It has performed for the annual Houston Festival, the Bellaire Antique Show, for charitable institutions, chambers of commerce, historical societies, and cattle auctions.[35]

In February 1983 the band played its third successive engagement for the McKellar Ranch Herd Foundation at the Astro Village Lodge ballroom. The auction featured the sale of red Brahman females, and the band performed prior to the bidding. Music for this affair consisted mainly of rousing marches and peppy numbers designed to affect the cattlemen psychologically. Texas cattle barons seemed to bid more briskly after the pepping-up routine. The resounding tempo of Sousa's "Stars and Stripes Forever," the tantalizing sound of "76 Trombones," and the rhythmic novelty of Hill's arrangement of "Hernando's Hideaway" may have programmed one booted Texas dude to bid $75,000 for a calf that would not have been a bargain at $50,000.[36]

The sprightly, melodic music of the Good Times Brass Band consists of marches, polkas, waltzes, pop tunes, medleys, and singalongs for which the words are included in the programs. Designed to appeal to the entire family, the concerts are especially appreciated by older listeners who enjoy the town band program concept. Usually at the conclusion, people tarry awhile to get their programs autographed and to exchange small talk with the conductor.

"It's a little like the preacher, after the sermon, remaining to shake hands with the congregation," Hill explains. "You'd be surprised at the number of people who tell you that they once played a horn." [37]

A highlight of 1983's "Concert in the Park" schedule was a performance sponsored by Bellaire jointly with the town's historical society and the Southwest Houston Chamber of Commerce. In preparation for the event, the Bellaire Chamber of Commerce sent out 10,000 fliers by direct mail in addition to advertising the concert as a public service-oriented function through the news media. To take care of the overflow attendance, a street adjacent to the park and a nearby parking lot were reserved. Park benches provided for some seating, but many people depended upon their own portable chairs and stools. Almost an hour before the opening number, the two areas were filled to capacity. Colors of the audience's casual attire added zest to the crisp autumn scene.

The program opened with "The Star-Spangled Banner" and closed with "Washington Post," a march by Sousa. Four singalongs spaced the program. These included "My Wild Irish Rose," "Bicycle Built for Two," "The Band Played On," and "America the Beautiful."

Instantaneous response to the music was demonstrated by the children patting their feet and skipping about and adults sashaying and marching around the gazebo to the tempo of the music. Asked to comment later, Hill said, "It's the way they identify with our music. The music projects happiness, and happiness releases inhibitions." [38]

At the close, the conductor and bandsmen welcomed those who wished to visit and collect autographs. One woman, the wife of a professional dance band leader, told Hill the music was the best jazz-swing she had ever heard a concert band play. Another told Hill that he had brought something special to Houston.

Conductor Hill would be the last one to admit it, but that "something special" is a vital part of his own legend that spirals as the years accumulate.

CBS Anchorman Dan Rather, photograph was made in 1980 and I understand it is a favorite of the journalist.

Sam Houston State University student Dan Rather in a serious mood.

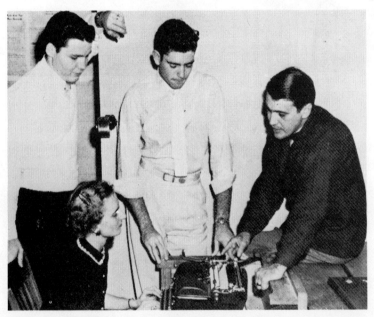

Dan Rather, editor of The Houstonian, *Sam Houston campus newspaper (center) and staff members and sponsor (right). Circa 1952–1953.*

BMOC (Big Man On Campus) Dan Rather during his senior year at Sam Houston State University in 1953.

Rather emcees campus bathing beauty contest in 1953. One of the judges crowns Miss Sam Houston State College — as the school was known then. The winner was Jeanelle Kingsbery of Brenham, Texas.

Rather (right) poses with other campus leaders at Sam Houston State University in 1952.

Rather treats a classmate to a hamburger. Uncle Ben's hamburger stand was an old converted bus at the edge of the Huntsville campus.

Novelist Jewel Gibson in the role of Phoebe Goolsby and actor Jerome Jordan in the role of Joshua Beene in the Alley Theatre production of Joshua Beene and God, *directed by the late Nina Vance in Houston, 1950.*

Novelist Jewel Gibson with Random House publisher Bennett Cerf (right) at autograph party celebrating the publication of her second novel, Black Gold.

Miss Patsy Woodall's first home in Huntsville was the Elkins Boardinghouse where she stayed in 1910. (This is a very rare picture of the old Victorian house long since torn down. It was also the birthplace of the billionaire, the late Judge Jim Elkins of Houston.)

Miss Patsy points to the shovel presented to her after the groundbreaking ceremonies for the Huntsville Memorial Hospital District in September 1977. The shovel occupies a conspicuous place on her trophy wall at Sunset Lake near Huntsville.

Miss Patsy is fond of cooking for her friends. Here she is preparing a festive meal at her cottage at Sunset Lake.

Monte Barrett, author of Smoke Up the Valley *and creator of the comic strip* Jane Arden, *and the author at a writers conference at the University of Oklahoma.*

Novelist-playwright Jewel Gibson, left, and Martha Anne Turner.

J. Evetts Haley and Strawberry, his favorite cutting horse.

TEXAS WESTERN PRESS

THE UNIVERSITY OF TEXAS AT EL PASO
EL PASO, TEXAS
79999

November 30, 1971

Miss Martha Anne Turner
Department of English
Sam Houston State University
Huntsville, Texas 77340

Dear Miss Turner:

Last week I took the complete Yellow Rose home and read in bed without interruption. Perhaps I should say I went to bed with the Yellow Rose but I am too old for that.

I found the complete package very interesting and easy reading. I think Texana collectors will go for this item. As far as I know nothing much has been done on the Yellow Rose.

We are going to get 250 copies bound hardback. Don't know if we can get them before Christmas, but will try.

Sincerely yours,

Carl Hertzog

Photograph of letter from Carl Hertzog to Martha Anne Turner.

Carl Hertzog, left, former director of Texas Western Press (University of Texas at El Paso) and author-editor C. L. Sonnichsen. The two teamed to produce Sonnichsen's Pass of the North.

C. L. Sonnichsen with Mount Franklin in the background.

Walter Prescott Webb, longtime University of Texas professor and historian of national magnitude.

Photograph by Neal Douglas

Charles Lee Hill and The Good Times Brass Band

Conductor Charles Lee Hill and the Good Times Brass Band after a concert at Bellaire Community Center dedicating the gazebo, October 16, 1983. First row, from left (kneeling): Kathy Beck, Joe Aguilar, Glenna Fought, Bill Callender, Barbara Hoope, Bill House, Wayne Baker, Ben Budd; second row (standing): Conductor Hill, James Rhode, James Pinto, Suzi Paxton, Donna Moran, Cindy Metcalfe, Drew Klomann, Mac Caldwell; third row: Joe Gallo, Bill Burkett, Jr., Sam Graves, Bill Burkett, Sr., Willis Jacus, Al Schuttenberg, Noah Lee, Art Newman, Gene Markley, Bill Callender, Jr., John Roy, and Biff Clifford.

Good Times Brass Band playing for Bellaire Folk Festival, at the Bellaire Community Center, Houston 1982.

Trumpet section of the Houstonians, Sam Houston State University dance orchestra directed by Hill in the 1940s. Note the brass derbies which were used to muffle the tone of the instrument and achieve the do-wah effect which jazzman Hill introduced and perfected in his arrangements.

Hill at the age of thirty-seven, directing his jazz orchestra at Sam Houston State University.

Terrell and Walter Prescott Webb at their home in Austin in 1963.
Photograph by Charles Smith

Mody Boatright, folklorist, editor, and University of Texas professor.

Endnotes

DAN RATHER

1. Dan Rather with Mickey Herskowitz, *The Camera Never Blinks: Adventures of a TV Journalist* (New York: William Morrow and Company, Inc., 1977), 45, 53–55 *passim*.

2. *Ibid.*, 44–53, 55–57.

3. Norma Dell Monk (ed.), "Dan Rather New Anchorman for CBS," *Alumnus*, Sam Houston State University, 54 (Spring 1980), 24.

4. Dan Rather biographical file, Archives, Sam Houston State University Library. See also Rather, *The Camera Never Blinks,* 111–129, 134–140, 142–148.

5. Monk, "Dan Rather New Anchorman for CBS," 24.

6. Chris Stoehr, "Dan Rather says he won't chain himself to the CBS anchor desk," *Houston Post*, February 25, 1980.

7. Official government transcript, March 19, 1974, Houston, Texas. Accounts of this confrontation were exposed in the national news media and aired by all major TV networks. The best reportage is Rather's own "Prologue: Houston: Home Again," in *The Camera Never Blinks,* 1–24.

8. *Ibid.* See also official government transcript, March 19, 1974, Houston, Texas.

9. Tracy Gupton, "Dan Rather: From the Piney Woods to Broadway," *the Raven,* I (Spring-Summer 1981), 12–16.

10. Tom Shales, "Rather may be locked in feudal war after he assumes CBS News throne," *Dallas Morning News,* March 14, 1980.

11. Files for *The Houstonian,* Sam Houston State University newspaper, 1950–1954, and *The Alcalde,* Sam Houston State University yearbook, 1950–1954, Archives, Sam Houston State University Library.

12. Rather, *The Camera Never Blinks,* 29.

13. Official records, Texas A&M University Athletic Department, College Station.

14. Rather, *The Camera Never Blinks,* 31, 33. See also Gupton, "Dan Rather: From the Piney Woods to Broadway," *the Raven,* I (Spring-Summer 1981), 13. Rather's inability to make Puny Wilson's Bearkat football team was his only failure.

15. Rather's background is common knowledge. He has never tried to conceal the fact that his father, Irvin Rather, worked for a pipeline construction company or that his mother waited tables before her marriage.

16. *The Huntsville Item* files, 1952–1954, Archives, Sam Houston State University Library. See also Rather, *The Camera Never Blinks,* 34–38 *passim*, 136.

17. Rather, *The Camera Never Blinks,* 37.

18. Official records, Registrar's Office, Sam Houston State University, Huntsville, Texas.

19. Jerry Urban, "Rather Worked at Being Tough," *The Huntsville Item,* front page, March 8, 1981. All biographical sources carry the water tower incident.

20. Dan Rather, "The Sale," *Horizon* 4 (Fall 1950), 18–20.

21. Rather writes pretty much as he talks. Both of his books are excellent illustrations of this characteristic.

22. Program, Sam Houston State University Distinguished Alumni Dinner, Criminal Justice Center, October 21, 1977.

23. Norma Dell Monk, executive director, Sam Houston State University Alumni Association, to Martha Anne Turner, January 5, 1981.

24. Susan Schackman, assistant to Dan Rather, CBS News, to Martha Anne Turner, January 15, 1981.

25. Interview with Dan Rather, October 15, 1980. See also Jerry Urban, "Dan Rather laid back — no way!" *The Houstonian* 68 (October 30, 1980), 8.

26. Janis Parks, "Team captain Rather at ease with scrutiny," *Houston Post*, June 16, 1981. See also "The Houston Hurricane: Dan Rather is a country boy in a hurry," *Time* 115 (February 25, 1980), 72–75.

27. Ann Hodges, "Dan Rather wants to be known as the man who cares about what he's doing," *Houston Chronicle*, June 17, 1981.

28. From my own memory of Carla. For Rather's corroboration, see *The Camera Never Blinks*, 40–51 *passim*.

29. "Station Break," *Houston Post*, August 6, 1981.

30. Sally Bedell, "Dan Rather's Dilemma," *TV Guide* 29 (May 30–June 5, 1981), 28.

31. Dan Rather, "Pressure: How to keep going when the going gets tough," *Ladies Home Journal*, Vol. C, No. 4 (April 1983), 57.

32. Rather, *The Camera Never Blinks*, 53.

33. "The New Face of TV News: Dan Rather becomes CBS's $8 million man as network journalism booms," *Time* 115 (February 25, 1980), 64.

34. *Ibid.*

35. *Ibid.* See also "The Houston Hurricane: Dan Rather is a country boy in a hurry," *Time* 115 (February 25, 1980), 72–75.

JEWEL GIBSON

1. Paul Crume, "Rustic Religious Dictator Sharply Seen by Texas Author," *Dallas Morning News*, September 22, 1946.

2. *Ibid.*

3. J. Frank Dobie, "Writing That Has Vitality," *Chicago Daily Sun*, October 13, 1946.

4. Anne Calhoun, "Messiah Beene Is Texas Truth Stranger Than Most Fiction," *Dallas Times-Herald*, October 12, 1946.

5. *Ibid.*

6. "Lord's Appointed," *Houston Chronicle*, September 15, 1946.

7. *Ibid.*

8. Thomas Sugrue, "Center of the University," *New York Herald Tribune*, October 13, 1946.

9. *Ibid.*

10. Phil Stong, "Old Man of the Tribe," *Saturday Review of Literature*, October 13, 1946.

11. "Fiction at Home and Abroad," *New York Times*, November 9, 1946.

12. Pamela Hansford Johnson, "Review of *Joshua Beene And God*," *John O'London's Weekly*, October 15, 1949.

13. As related by Jewel Gibson. See also Melvin Mason, "The Girl with the Blue-Handled Hoe . . . ," *Texas College English*, III (October 1968), np.

14. J. Frank Dobie, *Guide to Life and Literature of the Southwest* (Dallas: Southern Methodist University Press, 1952), revised edition, 4.

15. Jan Harold Brunvand, *The Study of American Folklore* (New York: W. W. Norton Company, 1968), 103–105.

16. Walter Prescott Webb and others (eds.), *The Handbook of Texas*, 3 vols. (Austin: Texas State Historical Association, 1952 and 1976), 1:102.

17. Alta Rae Reagan, "Bald Prairie Cemetery," "Bald Prairie Church of Christ," and "History of the Bald Prairie Church of Christ," original typescripts in Gibson collection, np.

18. Webb, et al., *The Handbook of Texas*, 2:488.

19. Richard M. Dorson, *America in Legend* (New York: Pantheon Books, 1973), 11–14.

20. *Ibid.*, 17–28 *passim*.

21. Jewel Gibson, *Joshua Beene And God* (New York: Random House, 1946), first American edition, 10.

22. *Ibid.*, 10–11.

23. *Ibid.*, 8.

24. *Ibid.*, 14.

25. Jewel Gibson to Martha Anne Turner, August 18, 1976. Letter.

26. Gibson to Turner, September 29, 1976. Letter.

27. Gibson, *Joshua Beene And God*, 5.

28. *Ibid.*, 9.

29. *Ibid.*, 38.

30. "Author Would Clean All 'Spring Creeks,' " *Texas Week* (September 28, 1946), 33–34.

31. Jewel Gibson to Martha Anne Turner, November 15, 1976. Private interview.

J. Evetts Haley

1. Walter S. Campbell, *The Book Lover's Southwest: A Guide to Good Reading* (Norman: Oklahoma University Press, 1955), 187–188. See also J. Evetts Haley and XIT Ranch files, Panhandle-Plains Historical Society, Canyon, Texas.

2. J. Evetts Haley, *The XIT Ranch of Texas and the Early Days of the Llano Estacado*, with Introduction by John V. Farwell (Chicago: The Lakeside Press, 1929). Two copies, Sam Houston State University Library.

3. "The starting place is naturally enough with J. Frank Dobie, who vies with J. Evetts Haley as the man who looks most like a writer of Western subjects ought to" — Joe B. Frantz and Julian Ernest Choate, Jr., *American Cowboy: The Myth and the Reality* (Norman: University of Oklahoma Press, 1955), 178–179.

4. Chandler A. Robinson, "J. Evetts Haley in Perspective," *The J. Evetts Haley Roundup*, Catalogue Seven, Betty Smedley, Bookseller (El Paso: Guynes Printing Company, January 1974), 1. See also biographical file, Barker Texas History Center, University of Texas at Austin.

5. J. Evetts Haley, "Betty and Her Books," *Ranges of Grass and the Men on Horseback*, Catalogue Eleven, Betty Smedley Rare Books (Austin: Crawford-Penick, Inc., 1976), 3.

6. *Ibid.*

7. J. Evetts Haley, *Jeff Milton: A Good Man with a Gun* (Norman: Oklahoma University Press, 1948), ix.

8. Dave Shanks, "A Salty Texas Rebel," Chandler A. Robinson (ed.), *J. Evetts Haley and the Passing of the Old West* (Austin: Jenkins Publishing Company, 1978), 61.

9. J. Evetts Haley to Martha Anne Turner, June 21, 1950.

10. Haley, *The XIT Ranch of Texas* . . . (Norman: Oklahoma Press, 1953), vii.

11. *Ibid.*

12. *Ibid.*, 6–17 *passim*.

13. *Ibid.*, "The State Capitol and Its Builders," 52–53.

14. *Ibid.*, "Fences, Windmills, and 'Barbecue's' Bad Men," 75, 88, 98, 103. See also Cordia Sloan Duke and Joe B. Frantz, *6,000 Miles of Fence: Life on the XIT Ranch of Texas* (Austin: University of Texas Press, 1961), 98–116 *passim*.

15. Haley, *The XIT Ranch of Texas* . . . , 161–181.

16. *Ibid.*, 49–57; 88ff; 224–226. See also Campbell, *The Book Lover's Southwest*, 187–188; Duke and Frantz, *6,000 Miles of Fence*, 3–4, 108, 176, 199.

17. Haley, *Jeff Milton: A Good Man with a Gun*, ix.

18. Robinson, *J. Evetts Haley and the Passing of the Old West*, 32. On *Charles Goodnight* see also Mabel Major and others, *Southwest Heritage: A Literary History* (Albuquerque: The University of New Mexico Press, 1948), 109, and J. Frank Dobie, *Guide to Life and Literature of the Southwest* (Dallas: Southern Methodist University Press, 1952), 104.

19. Evetts Haley, Jr., "Preface: A Few Words From and About My Father," *J. Evetts Haley and the Passing of the Old West*, 19.

20. Joseph Warren, "Suppression of a Book," *J. Evetts Haley and the Passing of the Old West*, 113–114. See also Walter Trohan, "Texan's Book on Johnson is Still at Top," *Chicago Tribune*, October 16, 1964: "Haley's detractors have made no attempt to answer his charges. Instead they have centered their fire on Haley, calling him a hate-monger and a crackpot in published reports and worse in whispering campaigns."

21. Robinson, "J. Evetts Haley in Perspective," *The J. Evetts Haley Roundup*, 3.

22. The interview appears in *The Congressional Record* (September 1964), A4550-A4551.

23. Joe B. Frantz, "Memoirs On J. Evetts Haley," *J. Evetts Haley and the Passing of the Old West*, 126.

24. *Ibid.*

CARL HERTZOG AND E. H. ANTONE

1. Martha Anne Turner, Hertzog-Antone correspondence.

2. E. H. Antone to Martha Anne Turner, February 9, 1972.

3. Evan Haywood Antone, "Texas Western Press: The First Twenty-Five Years," brochure, Texas Western Press (September 1977), 1.

4. Al Lowman, "Carl Hertzog, Printer," *Printer at the Pass: The Work of Carl Hertzog* (San Antonio: The University of Texas Institute of Texan Cultures, 1972), v-x.

5. Antone, "Texas Western Press: The First Twenty-Five Years," 5. See also catalog items in *Printer at the Pass* and William R. Holman, "A Hertzog Dozen," xiii-xix.

6. Betty Smedley, *A Carl Hertzog Hope Chest*, limited edition, copy no. 93 (Austin: Crawford-Penick, Inc., September 1972), 25 pp.

7. Lowman, "Carl Hertzog, Printer," and Holman, "A Hertzog Dozen" in *Printer at the Pass*, v-x, xiii-xix. See also Carl Hertzog, "Geometry and Typography," *The Craftsman*, March 1924; "Dynamic Typography," *The Inland Printer*, December 1924; and "The Composing Stick as a Paint Brush," *The Inland Printer*, July 1926.

8. Antone, ". . . The First Twenty-Five Years," 2.

9. *Ibid.*, 3.

10. Carl Hertzog, "Tribute to C. L. Sonnichsen — As an Author," *Password* (El Paso County Historical Society) 16 (Winter 1971), 151. See also Dale L. Walker, *C. L. Sonnichsen: Grassroots Historian* (El Paso: Texas Western Press, 1972), 79.

11. Evan Haywood Antone, vita provided to author, May 11, 1981.

12. Carl Hertzog to Martha Anne Turner, May 8, 1981.

13. C. L. Sonnichsen to Martha Anne Turner, April 28, 1981. See also Evan Haywood Antone, vita.

14. Carl Hertzog to Martha Anne Turner, May 8, 1981.

15. Antone, ". . . The First Twenty-Five Years," 3–4. See also Catalogs of the School of Mines and Metallurgy, 1910 to 1944, Archives, the University of Texas at El Paso, and Walter P. Webb and others (eds.), *The Handbook of Texas* (Austin: Texas State Historical Association, 1952), 2:766–767.

16. Joyce Gibson Roach, *C. L. Sonnichsen* (Western Writers Series, no. 40; Boise, Idaho: Boise State University, 1979), 10. See also Walker, *C. L. Sonnichsen: Grassroots Historian*, 22.

17. C. L. Sonnichsen to Martha Anne Turner, April 29, 1981. See also Antone, vita.

18. Antone, ". . . The First Twenty-Five Years," 5.

19. *Ibid.*, 4. See also Antone, vita.

20. *Ibid.*

21. *Ibid.*

22. E. H. Antone to Martha Anne Turner, April 15, 1981.

23. E. H. Antone to Martha Anne Turner, May 20, 1981.

C. L. SONNICHSEN

1. Typescript provided author by C. L. Sonnichsen, April 28, 1981.

2. Joyce Gibson Roach, *C. L. Sonnichsen* (Western Writers Series, no. 40; Boise, Idaho: Boise State University, 1979), 11.

3. Dale L. Walker, *C. L. Sonnichsen: Grassroots Historian* (Monograph No. 34, Southwestern Studies; El Paso: Texas Western Press, 1972), 24, 25.

4. C. L. Sonnichsen, "The Poetry of History," *The American West* 12 (September 1975), 27.

5. Walker, *C. L. Sonnichsen: Grassroots Historian*, 15–16.

6. *Ibid.*, 24. See also Roach, *C. L. Sonnichsen*, 8.

7. Walker, *C. L. Sonnichsen: Grassroots Historian*, 22–24 *passim*; typescript provided author, April 28, 1981.

8. Walker, *C. L. Sonnichsen: Grassroots Historian*, 31.

9. Roach, *C. L. Sonnichsen*, 10. See also Walker, *C. L. Sonnichsen: Grassroots Historian*, 22.

10. C. L. Sonnichsen, *The Southwest in Life and Literature* (New York: The Devin-Adair Company, 1962), 9ff. Note also Dedication and Contents.

11. C. L. Sonnichsen, "The Grassroots Historian," *The Southwestern Historical Quarterly* 73 (January 1970), 381. See also *The Chicago Tribune*, August 6, 1960, and Roach, *C. L. Sonnichsen*, 9.

12. C. L. Sonnichsen, "Blood on the Typewriter," *The Grave of John Wesley Hardin: Three Essays on Grassroots History* (College Station: Texas A&M University Press, 1979), 22–26 *passim*.

13. G. M. Panowich, "Famous Texas Feuds," *Houston Chronicle Magazine*, December 7, 1958.

14. Sonnichsen typescript, April 28, 1981. See also Walker, *C. L. Sonnichsen: Grassroots Historian*, 31.

15. *Ibid.*

16. Sonnichsen, "The Grassroots Historian," 3. See also "Blood on the Typewriter," as cited, 25.

17. C. L. Sonnichsen, *Outlaw: Bill Mitchell alias Baldy Russell* (Denver: Sage Books, 1965), 173. See also "Blood on the Typewriter," as cited above, and Walker, *C. L. Sonnichsen: Grassroots Historian*, 31–34 *passim*.

18. *Ibid.*

19. Sonnichsen typescript, April 28, 1981.

20. C. L. Sonnichsen to Martha Anne Turner, June 6, 1981.

21. Walter Prescott Webb and others (eds.), *The Handbook of Texas* (Austin: Texas State Historical Association, 1952), 1:129–130.

22. Sonnichsen, *Roy Bean: Law West of the Pecos* (New York: Macmillan Company, 1943), 18, 54. See also Roach, *C. L. Sonnichsen*, 12–13 *passim*.

23. *The Chicago Tribune*, September 4, 1958. See also Walker, *C. L. Sonnichsen: Grassroots Historian*, 54–55.

24. J. Frank Dobie, *Guide to Life and Literature of the Southwest* (Dallas: Southern Methodist University Press, revised edition, 1952), 68. See also Walter S. Campbell, *The Book Lover's Southwest: A Guide to Good Reading* (Norman: University of Oklahoma Press, 1955), 75.

25. Statement made to author by C. L. Sonnichsen, April 28, 1981.

26. *Ibid.* See also Roach, *C. L. Sonnichsen,* 19, for emphasis on Sonnichsen's total dedication to the Southwest, its literature, and its culture.

27. C. L. Sonnichsen to Martha Anne Turner, April 28, 1981. See also C. L. Sonnichsen, *Cowboys and Cattle Kings* (Norman: University of Oklahoma Press, 1950), xvii.

28. *Saturday Review of Literature,* June 16, 1951.

29. *American Historical Review* 56 (January 1951), 365–366.

30. C. L. Sonnichsen, "The Folklore of Texas Feuds," *Observations and Reflections on Texas Folklore,* Publications of the Texas Folklore Society (Austin: Encino Press, 1972), 35. See also "The Theory and Practice of Feuding: An Introduction," in C. L. Sonnichsen, *I'll Die Before I'll Run* (New York: Harper & Brothers Publishers, 1951), x-xviii; "Blood on the Typewriter" and "The Grassroots Historian," as cited.

31. Sonnichsen, *Outlaw: Bill Mitchell alias Baldy Russell,* 20. Typescript statement provided author: "In the 1960s he published books on a variety of subjects [including] a biography of Bill Mitchell, alias Baldy Russell, who was on the dodge for forty years and was so tough that he died standing up in a Douglas hospital."

32. "El Paso," *Encyclopaedia Britannica* (London: Encyclopaedia Britannica, Inc., William Benton Publisher, 1969), 8:301.

33. Evan Haywood Antone, "Texas Western Press: The First Twenty-Five Years," brochure, Texas Western Press (September 1977), 4–5. See also "Book-Makers at the Pass" in this volume.

34. C. L. Sonnichsen vita provided the author for this sketch, June 19, 1981. See also Texas Western Press, The University of Texas at El Paso, Booklist 1981, "Announcing! *Pass of the North* by C. L. Sonnichsen," back of front cover and page 1.

Originally scheduled for release in 1980, *Pass of the North,* Volume I (1529–1917) was delayed until the historian could prepare a sequel, Volume II (1918–1980) to pair with it. Designed by Evan Haywood Antone, the second volume begins with the effects of World War I on El Paso and ends with the emergence of El Paso-Juarez as a major international metropolis celebrating four centuries on the Rio Grande.

35. Sonnichsen vita as previously cited. See also Walker, *C. L. Sonnichsen: Grassroots Historian,* 83–84.

36. Inscription for the Medallion of Merit, Sonnichsen files. See also Walker, *C. L. Sonnichsen: Grassroots Historian,* 84.

37. Sonnichsen, "The Little Blue Flame," *Nova,* The University of Texas at El Paso Magazine 7 (October 1972), 11–17.

38. Sonnichsen vita. See also C. L. Sonnichsen, "Western Fiction: Index to America" in *From Hopalong to Hud: Thoughts on Western Fiction* (College Station: Texas A&M University Press, 1978), 3–8 *passim.*

39. Bud Newman, *The Writings of C. L. Sonnichsen,* a bibliography prepared for *C. L. Sonnichsen: Grassroots Historian,* 93–99. See also Sonnichsen vita.

40. Sonnichsen, "Tombstone in Fiction," *The Journal of Arizona History* 8 (Summer 1968), 58.

41. Sonnichsen, "Western Fiction: Index to America" *From Hopalong to Hud,* 4.

42. *Ibid.,* 7.

43. Sonnichsen, "Sex on the Lone Prairee," *From Hopalong to Hud,* 100.

44. *Ibid.,* 167.

45. Sonnichsen, "From Hopalong to Hud: The Unheroic Cowboy in Western Fiction," *From Hopalong to Hud,* 104.

46. *Ibid.,* 105.

47. *Ibid.,* 119.

48. *Ibid.,* 117.

49. *Ibid.,* 125.

50. *Ibid.,* 126. See also Philip French, *Westerns* (New York: Viking, 1974), 142.

51. Sonnichsen, "Western Fiction: Index to America," *From Hopalong to Hud,* 5.

52. Sonnichsen,. "The Grave of John Wesley Hardin," *The Grave of John Wesley Hardin: Three Essays . . .* , 60.

53. Sonnichsen, "Blood on the Typewriter," *The Grave of John Wesley Hardin: Three Essays . . .* , 18–21 *passim.* See also previous reference.

54. *Ibid.*, 15.

55. *Ibid.*, 32. The feuding story that climaxed in 1911 at the village of Coahama is still unpublished.

56. Sonnichsen, "Blood on the Typewriter," *The Grave of John Wesley Hardin: Three Essays . . .* , 33. See also Sonnichsen, "The Grassroots Historian," 391.

57. Sonnichsen, "Blood on the Typewriter," *The Grave of John Wesley Hardin: Three Essays . . .* , 33.

58. *Ibid.*, 33. See also "The Grassroots Historian," *Nova,* The University of Texas at El Paso Magazine 5 (Summer 1970), 5.

59. Sonnichsen, "The Poetry of History," 27.

60. *Ibid.*, 60: "Call no man historian unless he makes you feel."

61. Sonnichsen, "Blood on the Typewriter," *The Grave of John Wesley Hardin: Three Essays . . .* , 33–35 *passim.*

WALTER PRESCOTT WEBB

1. Wilson M. Hudson, "Webb My Teacher" in *Three Men in Texas,* Ronnie Dugger, (ed.) (Austin: University of Texas Press, 1967), 128.

2. *Ibid.* The incident had a salutary effect on Webb. When nervous doctoral candidates appeared before him for their orals, he put them at ease and asked the type questions that permitted them to reveal their knowledge. As the article develops, there will be additional detail on this point.

3. Joe B. Frantz, "Webb, Walter Prescott," *The Handbook of Texas: A Supplement,* Vol. 3, Eldon Stephen Branda, (ed.) (Austin: Texas State Historical Association, 1976), 1091.

4. Lon Tinkle, "Meetings in Dallas" in *Three Men in Texas,* 144.

5. Branda (ed.), *The Handbook of Texas,* 3:1090.

6. W. P. Webb, "The Texan's Story," Walter Prescott Webb Collection, Barker Texas History Center, The University of Texas at Austin, Box 2M245, 18ff. See also "Autobiography" same citation.

7. *Ibid.*

8. Joe B. Frantz, "Walter Prescott Webb: 'He'll Do to Ride the River With' " in Walter Prescott Webb, *An Honest Preface and Other Essays* (Boston: Houghton Mifflin Company, 1959), 15.

9. Walter Prescott Webb, "The Search for William E. Hinds," *Harper's Magazine* 223 (July 1961), 62.

10. Mrs. C. P. Jones, "My Unforgettable Pupil," C. B. Smith Collection of Walter Prescott Webb Papers, Archives, Texas State Library, Austin, Box 2-22/793.

11. Walter Prescott Webb, *The Great Frontier* (Austin: University of Texas Press, 1952), 406.

12. Frantz, "Walter Prescott Webb: 'He'll Do to Ride the River With,' " 4–6 *passim.*

13. Webb, "The Search for William E. Hinds," 64.

14. *Ibid.* See also Frantz, "Walter Prescott Webb: 'He'll Do to Ride the River With,' " 7. Of the various accounts I've read, Frantz's is by far the best.

15. Webb, "The Search for William E. Hinds," 64.

16. Frantz, "Walter Prescott Webb: 'He'll Do to Ride the River With,' " 7.

17. Necah Stewart Furman, *Walter Prescott Webb: His Life and Impact* (Albuquerque: The University of New Mexico Press), 27. See also Webb, "The Texan's Story," as cited, 71.

18. Webb, "The Search for William E. Hinds," 65.

19. *Ibid.*, 66.

20. *Ibid.*

21. Webb, "The Texan's Story," 106. See also "Autobiography."

22. Furman, *Walter Prescott Webb: His Life and Impact*, 40.

23. Webb, "The Search for William E. Hinds," 67.

24. *Ibid.*

25. Frantz, "Walter Prescott Webb: 'He'll Do to Ride the River With,' " 13.

26. Walter Prescott Webb, "History as High Adventure" in *An Honest Preface and Other Essays* (Boston: Houghton Mifflin Company, 1959), 201.

27. *Ibid.*, 202.

28. Webb, "The Historical Seminar" in *An Honest Preface*, 167.

29. Webb, "History as High Adventure" in *An Honest Preface*, 206. See also Webb, *The Great Frontier*, 406.

30. Hudson, "Webb My Teacher," *Three Men in Texas*, 128.

31. Furman, *Walter Prescott Webb: His Life and Impact*, 82–83.

32. *Ibid.*

33. Webb to Charles Ramsdell, July 22, 1923, Walter Prescott Webb Collection, Barker Texas History Center, University of Texas at Austin, Box 2M259.

34. Webb, "History as High Adventure" in *An Honest Preface*, 203.

35. *Ibid.* The University of Chicago tried to redeem itself by inviting Webb to teach there in the summer of 1947. He declined. He accepted the honorary doctor of laws degree the university conferred upon him on December 19, 1958. The university withheld the letter informing him of the honor until they had confirmation of his acceptance by telephone.

36. *Ibid.*, 208.

37. Frantz, "Walter Prescott Webb: 'He'll Do to Ride the River With,' " 46.

38. Walter Prescott Webb, *The Texas Rangers* (Boston: Houghton Mifflin Company, 1935), ix.

39. Hudson, "Webb My Teacher," *Three Men in Texas*, 127.

40. Webb, "History as High Adventure" in *An Honest Preface*, 209–210.

41. Webb, *The Great Frontier*, 407–408.

42. Webb, "History as High Adventure" in *An Honest Preface*, 210.

43. *Ibid.*, 213.

44. Webb, *The Great Frontier*, 409. The statement is peculiar to Webb's modesty. As thorough and painstaking as Webb was, he did not devote sixteen years to an introduction that exeeded 400 pages of meticulously documented material.

45. John Haller, "A Most Generous Offer" in *Three Men in Texas*, 94–96.

46. Glen L. Evans, "Free of Both Hate and Fear" in *Three Men in Texas*, 150–151. See also Walter Prescott Webb, "Dear Bedi," same citation, 83–85.

47. John Fischer, tribute to Webb in "A Man, His Land, and His Work," *the Graduate Journal* 6 (Winter 1964), 35–37.

48. W. P. Webb, "Texas Collection," *Southwestern Historical Quarterly* 51 (January 1948), 259–260.

49. W. P. Webb, "Down to the Texas Sea," Jenkins Garrett Collection of Walter Prescott Webb Papers, Library, University of Texas at Arlington, Division of Special Collections, Arlington, Texas, Box 21.

50. John Haller, "A Most Generous Offer" in *Three Men in Texas*, 97.

51. Walter Prescott Webb, "I Have Known Frank Dobie for about Thirty-five Years" in *Three Men in Texas*, 253–254.

52. Walter Prescott Webb, "Texas Collection," *Southwestern Historical Quarterly* 46 (1942–1943), 60, 70–71. See also *Kyle News*, April 20, 1920.

53. T. U. Taylor, "Johnson Institute," *Frontier Times*, February 1941.

54. Branda (ed.), *The Handbook of Texas*, 3:316.

55. Glen L. Evans, "Free of Both Hate and Fear" in *Three Men in Texas*, 149.

56. J. Frank Dobie, "Walter Prescott Webb," *Out of the Old Rock*, with a Preface by Bertha McKee Dobie (Boston: Little, Brown and Company, 1972), 60.

57. Frantz, "Walter Prescott Webb: 'He'll Do to Ride the River With,' " 34.

58. Roy Bedichek, *Adventures with a Texas Naturalist* (Austin: University of Texas Press, 1947), xix. The work was reissued in paperback in 1980.

59. *Ibid.*, xxii. See also Stanley Walker, "The Lively Hermit of Friday Mountain," *Saturday Evening Post*, October 16, 1948.

60. In his posthumous letter to Bedichek, which first appeared in a memorial issue of *The Observer* and later in *Three Men in Texas* (p. 85), Webb wrote: "It is possible you have conferred immortality on Friday Mountain and that in the future students and curious tourists in search of culture will make pilgrimages there to see where the Texas naturalist wrote his first book."

61. John Fischer, "An Unfashionable Kind of Historian" in *Three Men in Texas*, 112.

62. Webb, "The Search for William E. Hinds," 68.

63. Furman, *Walter Prescott Webb: His Life and Impact*, 130. The estrangement of the Webbs was exacerbated when he was Harkness lecturer in American history at London University in 1938. At that time the couple argued, and Jane called her husband a coward.

64. Webb, "The Search for William E. Hinds," 62.

65. Ellen Slayden to Maury Maverick, September 9, 1915, "General Correspondence, 1912–1918," Maury Maverick Papers, Barker Texas History Center, University of Texas at Austin. See also letter dated October 10, 1915, same citation.

66. Richard B. Henderson, *Maury Maverick: A Political Biography* (Austin: University of Texas Press, 1970), 18–21. On relationship between Maury Maverick and Ellen Slayden, see 25, 29, same citation.

67. Henderson, *Maury Maverick: A Political Biography*, on career, 51–53, 61–62, 116–122, 175–187, 190–192; on writings, 142–143, 208–210. See also Maury Maverick, *A Maverick American* (New York: Covici, Friede, 1937) and Maury-Slayden-Maverick Family Papers, Barker Texas History Center, University of Texas at Austin.

68. Ellen Maury Slayden, *Washington Wife: Journal of Ellen Maury Slayden from 1897–1919* (New York: Harper & Row, 1962), 54.

69. *Ibid.*, 280.

70. *Ibid.*, 8.

71. Terrell Webb, Preface, *Washington Wife*, xxi.

72. *Ibid.*

73. Dobie, "Walter Prescott Webb" in *Out of the Old Rock*, 160.

74. Tinkle, "Meetings in Dallas" in *Three Men in Texas*, 140–141.

75. Dobie, "Walter Prescott Webb" in *Out of the Old Rock*, 159.

76. Evans, "Free of Both Hate and Fear" in *Three Men in Texas*, 151.

77. Walter Prescott Webb, Introduction, *Washington Wife*, xvi.

78. *Ibid.*, xvi–xvii.

79. Terrell Webb, Preface, *Washington Wife*, xix.

80. *Ibid.*, xxi.

81. Tinkle, "Meetings in Dallas" in *Three Men in Texas*, 145–146 *passim*.

82. Dobie, "For Years We Three Sat Together" in *Three Men in Texas*, 99.

83. Helen Yenne, "Dr. W. P. Webb Dies in Crash," *The Daily Texan*, March 10, 1963, Garrett Collection, University of Texas at Arlington. See also biographical file, Barker Texas History Center, University of Texas at Austin, for various newspaper accounts.

By proclamation of former Gov. John Connally, Webb is buried in the State Cemetery in Austin, which is also the resting place of his friends, Frank and Bertha Dobie.

A statement Terrell Webb made a few years ago seems appropriate to quote here: "It was in San Antonio that I met and married Maury Maverick, my husband for thirty-four magical years, and the father of my son Maury, and my daughter Terrelita.

"Now that my life has taken on an added facet as the widow of my great and delightful later husband, Walter Prescott Webb, I am amazed at how strong I feel, how sustained I am by my capacity to feel and understand the life around me . . ." — Terrell Maverick Webb, *Growing Up in Texas* (Austin: Encino Press, 1972), 24.

84. Dobie, "For Years We Three Sat Together" in *Three Men in Texas,* 102.

MODY BOATRIGHT

1. Walter Prescott Webb and others (eds.), *The Handbook of Texas,* (Austin: Texas State Historical Association, 1952), 1:378.

2. Ernest B. Speck, *Mody C. Boatright* (Austin: Steck-Vaughn, Southwest Writers Series, No. 38, 1971), 1.

3. Webb, et al., *The Handbook of Texas,* 2:153. See also *Texas Almanac: 1976–1977* (Dallas: *The Dallas Morning News*), 339.

4. The first person to write on Pecos Bill was Edward O'Reilly, whose "Saga of Pecos Bill" was published in *Century Magazine* for October 1923 (106: 827–833).

5. Mody C. Boatright, *Tall Tales from Texas Cow Camps* (Dallas: The Southwest Press, 1934), xxiv.

6. Speck, *Mody C. Boatright,* 1.

7. Mody C. Boatright, *Gib Morgan: Minstrel of the Oil Fields* (Austin: Texas Folklore Society, No. 20, 1945), 2–3.

8. Eldon Stephen Branda (ed.), *The Handbook of Texas: A Supplement,* Vol. 3 (Austin: Texas State Historical Association, 1976), 91.

9. James T. Bracher (comp.), *Analytical Index to Publications of the Texas Folklore Society,* Volumes 1-36 (Austin: Southern Methodist University Press, 1973), 170. See also *The Handbook of Texas,* 3:81; and Wayland D. Hand, *Eyes On Texas: Fifty Years of Folklore in the Southwest* (Austin: Texas Folklore Society, 1967), 4, 11, 12, 15–16, 19–20.

10. Ernest B. Speck (ed.), Introduction to *Mody Boatright, Folklorist* (Austin: University of Texas Press, 1973), xviv.

11. Hand, *Eyes on Texas* . . . , 11.

12. Boatright, *Tall Tales from Texas Cow Camps,* 85, 93.

13. J. Evetts Haley, "Boatright, Mody C., *Tall Tales from Texas Cow Camps,*" *Southwestern Historical Quarterly* 38 (January 1935), 230–233.

14. See both essays in Speck (ed.), *Mody Boatright, Folklorist,* 13ff and 163ff.

15. J. Frank Dobie, *Guide to Life and Literature of the Southwest* (Dallas: Southern Methodist University Press, 1952), 20.

16. Mody C. Boatright, *Folklore of the Oil Industry* (Dallas: Southern Methodist University Press, 1963), 191.

17. *Ibid.,* 177.

18. Boatright, *Gib Morgan: Minstrel of the Oil Fields,* 98–99.

19. Boatright, "Gib Morgan Among the Heroes," in *Mody Boatright, Folklorist,* 66–67.

20. Harry H. Ransom, biographical essay, *Mody Boatright, Folklorist,* xiii.

21. Boatright, "Folklore in a Literate Society," in *Mody Boatright, Folklorist,* 120.

22. Ransom, biographical essay, xiv.

23. Franklin J. Meine, *Tall Tales of the Southwest* (New York: Alfred A. Knopf, 1946), 6.

24. *Ibid.,* xv.

25. Ransom, biographical essay, xvii.

CHARLES LEE HILL

1. Donn Laurence Mills, letter to Charles Lee Hill, *The Instrumentalist,* January 1982.

2. Charles Lee Hill to Martha Anne Turner, interview, September 10, 1983.

3. Hill archival material and scrapbooks.

4. *Ibid.* See also *Who's Who in the South and Southwest,* 13th edition (1973–1974), and *Who Is Who in Music,* 1951.

5. *Ibid.*

6. "We are Making America Musical," *School Music Magazine,* Fall 1937.

7. Tom Overton, "Music Man/Houston school librarian brushes the dust off dormant career . . . ," *Houston Post,* March 6, 1983. See also Hill file of archival material.

8. *Ibid.*

9. Charles Lee Hill (composer), "Red Rhythm Valley," copyright transferred 1945 to Volkwein Bros. Inc., Pittsburgh, Pa. Original score provided by arranger-composer Hill. See also Hill files of archival material.

10. Overton, "Music Man . . ."

11. Original file of *Three Sheets to the Wind* in possession of Hill.

12. Charles Lee Hill (composer), "At the Gremlin Ball," Carl Fischer, Inc., New York, 1944. Original score in Hill collection. See also *ASCAP Biographical Dictionary, 1980,* and *Texas Composers,* compiled by Whittle Music Co., Dallas, 1955.

13. Col. George S. Howard, USAF (Ret.), "Jazz Composition Premiered After a 34-Year Interim," *The School Musician/Director & Teacher,* Vol. 51, No. 1 (August/September 1979), 20, 62.

14. *Ibid.,* 62.

15. *Ibid.*

16. Col. George S. Howard, USAF, *The Big Serenade* (Evanston, Illinois: The Instrumentalist Company, 1961), 43–45.

17. *Ibid.,* 49. See also Howard, "Jazz Composition Premiered . . . ,"

18. Howard, *The Big Serenade,* 138.

19. *Ibid.,* 140.

20. *Ibid.,* 141–142.

21. Ed J. Murphy, Jr., "Campus Is Jumpin' at S.H.S.T.C./Saxophonist Is Professor of Music," *Houston Post,* October 10, 1948. See also George Simon, "jazz goes to college," *Metronome* (September 1948), 18–20; *point and counterpoint* (November 1948).

22. Ed Murphy, "Campus Swing Band Also a Lab Outfit," *Down Beat* (January 28, 1949), 16.

23. Charles Lee Hill, "Dance Music in School Bands," *The Southwestern Musician,* Vol. 51, No. 13 (September 1951), 15. See also C. C. Springfield, "Swing Goes to College!" *Houston Chronicle Magazine,* nd, Hill scrapbook.

24. Murphy, ". . . Saxophonist Is Professor of Music."

25. Ed Cooper, "Houstonians Perform Thursday Night/Red-Hot Musical Program Lined Up by Hill's Outfit," *The Houstonian,* January 10, 1951.

26. *Band Music for the Sports Season,* Southern Music Company (catalogue), 1949–50 sport season, Box 358, San Antonio 6, Texas.

27. Overton, "Music Man . . ." See also Hill's collection of original scores.

28. Charles Lee Hill to Martha Anne Turner, interview, September 10, 1983.

29. *Ibid.*

30. Howard, "Jazz Composition Premiered . . . ," 62.

31. Marge Crumbaker, *Houston Post,* April 29, 1984; "Hill honored at 'Concert in the Park,' *The Daily Sentinel,* Nacogdoches, May 30, 1984; Stephen F. Austin State University Department of Bands, "Old Fashioned Park Concert," Pecan Acres Park, Sunday, April 29, 1984, 2:30 P.M. (program).

32. Mills, *The Instrumentalist,* January 1982.

33. Houston Good Times Band archives file provided author by Hill.

34. *Ibid.* "Donna Lee Brochure" provided by psychic.

35. Houston Good Times Brass Band archives file.

36. Charles Lee Hill to Martha Anne Turner, interview, February 25, 1983.

37. Hill to Turner, interview, October 20, 1983. See also Hill archival materials.

38. *Ibid.*

INDEX